POPE
JOHN PAUL II

Also by George Sullivan

SADAT: *The Man Who Changed Mid-East History*

STRANGE BUT TRUE STORIES OF WORLD WAR II

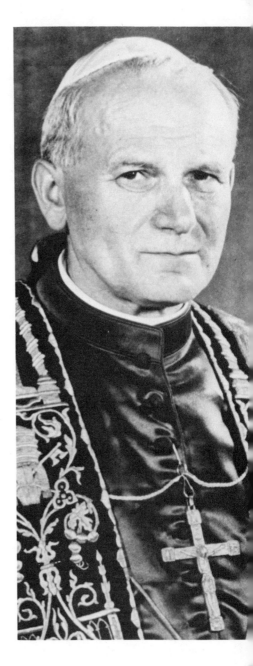

POPE
JOHN PAUL II
THE PEOPLE'S POPE

BY GEORGE SULLIVAN

Walker and Company
New York

First published in the United States of America
in 1984 by the Walker Publishing Company, Inc.

Published simultaneously in Canada by John Wiley & Sons
Canada, Limited, Rexdale, Ontario

Library of Congress Cataloging in Publication Data

Sullivan, George, 1927–
     Pope John Paul II.

     Bibliography: p.
     Includes index.
     Summary: A biography of Karol Wojtyla of Poland, the
first non-Italian to be elected Pope in several centuries.
     1. John Paul II, Pope, 1920–   —Juvenile literature.
2. Popes—Biography—Juvenile literature.   [1. John Paul
II, Pope, 1920–   .   2. Popes]   I. Title.   II. Title:
Pope John Paul 2.   III. Title: Pope John Paul Two.
BX1378.5.S85   1984   282′.092′4 [B] [92]   83-40395

ISBN: 0-8027-6523-8

Library of Congress Catalog Card Number: 83-40395

Book design by Robert Charles Bartosiewicz de la Vega

Printed in the United States of America

10 9 8 7 6 5 4 3 2 1

POPE
JOHN PAUL II

CHAPTER

1

ON THE LAST DAY OF HIS LIFE, POPE JOHN PAUL I FOL-
lowed the routine he had established for himself on his first
day in office. He awoke at five o'clock. He drank a cup of
coffee that had been placed in the corridor outside his
rooms in the Vatican Palace. Walking a few steps to his private chapel, he said mass, a celebration of the Lord's Supper, and the chief religious service of the Catholic Church.

He had breakfast in his private dining room, worked in
his bedroom until about eight, then took his private elevator to the floor below to begin his official day as the spiritual
ruler of the world's 740 million baptized Catholics, one sixth
of the world's population.

Except for lunch and his afternoon siesta, he remained
at his desk throughout the day. At seven-thirty he had his
usual daily meeting with Cardinal Jean Villot, the Vatican
Secretary of State. Pope John ended the day where it began, in his chapel with evening prayers.

1

He decided he would read in bed for a time. He chose a copy of Thomas Kempis's *Imitation of Christ.* He switched on his reading lamp.

Before daybreak the next morning, Vatican street cleaners saw the light coming from the pope's apartment. Perhaps they thought that the pope, like them, had already begun his working day.

Not long after five o'clock, a nun, following her daily ritual, placed a cup of coffee outside the doors of the pope's rooms. She was surprised when she returned at about five-thirty to retrieve the empty cup to find the coffee untouched. That had not happened once since John Paul I had been installed as pope several weeks before. But it was not for the nun to question the pope's routine. She returned to the kitchen without saying anything.

In the chapel, Father John Magee, private secretary to the pope, glanced at his watch. It was five-thirty. "Where is the pope?" he asked himself. He was always in the chapel by this time, preparing to say mass.

Father Magee waited for a few more minutes, then walked to the pope's bedroom and rapped at the door. There was no answer. He put his ear to the door. He heard nothing.

Father Magee entered the room. John Paul, propped up by pillows, was in a half-sitting position. In his hand he clutched several sheets of paper. His book was open beside him. The reading lamp was still burning.

The pope was dead. It seemed beyond belief. Only thirty-four days before, as Cardinal Albino Luciani, he had been elected pope. In that short span of time, he had begun to change the image of the office of the pope, or the papacy, as it is called. He had demonstrated how easily a pope can captivate the world with genuine personal warmth. He was beginning to be called "the smiling pope."

He had put his stamp on the office by refusing to accept the traditional tiara, or crown. He had rejected the use of the papal "we"; Pope John Paul preferred "I." It was simpler and more direct.

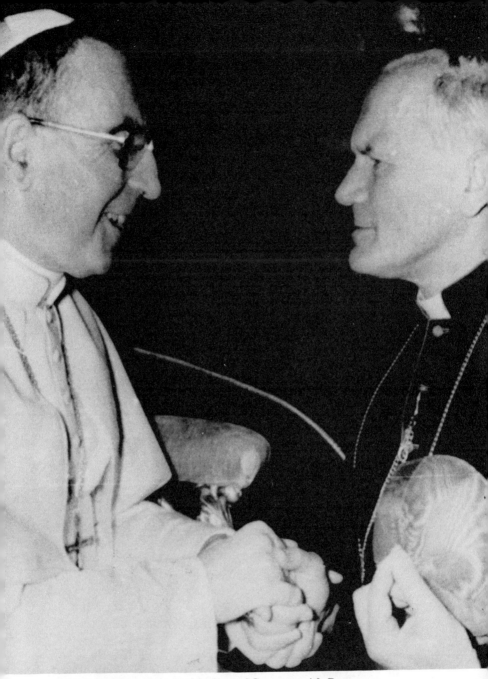

*Karol Wojtyla, then Archbishop of Cracow, with Pope
John Paul I in October 1978.
(United Press International)*

The shocked Father Magee immediately notified Cardinal Villot, who was at the pope's bedside in minutes to confirm that John Paul I was dead. His passing meant that Cardinal Villot would again assume the seat of authority and would hold that position until a new pope was elected.

Cardinal Villot summoned a physician, Dr. Renato Buzzonnetti, who established that John Paul had died of heart failure. Death had occurred around eleven o'clock the night before.

Word that the church was without a pope sped quickly through the hundreds of rooms and offices in the group of connected buildings that make up the Vatican Palace. Many people wept openly.

Catholics look upon the pope as the visible head of their church and believe that Jesus Christ established the office of the pope when he said to Simon, later to become St. Peter:

AND I SAY ALSO UNTO THEE, THAT THOU ART PETER, AND UPON THIS ROCK I WILL BUILD MY CHURCH, AND THE GATES OF HELL SHALL NOT PREVAIL AGAINST IT. (MATT. 16:18)

Catholics believe that the pope is infallible in matters concerning faith and morals. This means that they believe the pope cannot possibly commit an error when he speaks with papal authority on these subjects. His infallibility stems from the divine assistance given to the successors of St. Peter.

The pope has absolute authority in governing the church. He can make or dispense with church laws. He appoints cardinals and bishops, approves new religious orders, and establishes or divides church dioceses, or districts. He has the power to declare individuals as saints. He can excommunicate those who disobey his orders or church law; that is, he can cut them off from membership in the church.

Aside from his spiritual duties as head of the church, the pope also has governmental responsibilities. He is the ruler of Vatican City, an area of slightly more than 100 acres—a bit larger than New York's Central Park—within the city of Rome. Vatican City, with a population of about 1,000, is an independent state and, as such, has its own flag and stamps. Vatican City sends diplomatic representatives to 51 nations and receives diplomats from them.

Cardinal Albino Luciani, as John Paul I, was the 263rd successor to St. Peter. Like all popes, he was to have worn a ring, known as the fisherman's ring (St. Peter was a fisherman), which bore a seal engraved with an image of St. Peter as he was casting a net. Tradition dictates that when a break occurs in papal rule, the seal on the ring has to be broken. But John Paul had not been pope long enough for his ring to be made. There is also the custom of tapping the dead pope on the forehead three times with a silver hammer, calling out his name, and asking each time, "Are you dead?"

Cardinal Villot issued orders to close the massive bronze doors of St. Peter's Church, the biggest Christian church in the world. It stands above the crypt, or tomb, that is believed to contain the body of St. Peter. Built in the shape of a cross, with its massive dome designed by Michelangelo and dominating the skyline of Vatican City, St. Peter's represents the very heart of the Catholic Church. The doors of St. Peter's would not reopen until a new pope had been elected.

While doctors could quickly establish the medical reasons for the pope's heart failure, there was speculation that the awesome burdens of church leadership might have been a contributing factor. As spiritual head of the church, the pope must be in constant communication with the cardinals and others in the church who have roles as leaders. He must keep peace with the conservative elements who look upon change as a troubling force, while at the same time dealing in an effective manner with the liberal wing, which seeks to transform the church in many ways.

These battlelines were clearly drawn in the United States, where special problems beset the church. Many people blamed these problems on the Second Vatican Council, called by Pope John XXIII in 1962 to provide an updating of Catholic religious life and doctrine. In the fifteen or so years that had followed the closing of the council, the church had been thoroughly shaken. Weekly church attendance had declined. Huge numbers of Catholics were paying little or no attention to official church teachings on divorce or birth control and were acting accordingly. As many as one fifth of the American priests had left the active ministry, and an even higher percentage of nuns had withdrawn from religious life. Catholics would be expecting the new pope to end the years of crisis and confusion.

Cardinal Villot, the Vatican Secretary of State, knew all too well the procedures that had to be followed when a pope died. He had carried them out only two months before. Certain individuals had to be notified immediately. The first was Cardinal Carlo Confalonieri, the Dean of the Sacred College of Cardinals. The cardinals, who are appointed by the pope and act as his advisors, rank next to him in terms of authority within the church.

Cardinal Villot also supervised the preparation of the official Vatican statement announcing the pope's death. It read: "This morning, 29 September 1978, about five-thirty, the private secretary of the pope, contrary to custom not having found the Holy Father in the chapel of his private apartment, looked for him in his room and found him dead in bed with the light on, like one who was intent on reading. The physician, Dr. Renato Buzzonnetti, who hastened at once, verified the death as having presumably taken place around eleven o'clock yesterday evening through acute coronary thrombosis."

World leaders were informed through official channels. Within hours, the Vatican received messages of sympathy from Jimmy Carter, President of the United States; Leonid Breshnev, Premier of the Soviet Union; Queen Elizabeth II of England; and other heads of state.

Cardinal Villot also had to see to it that all the cardinals throughout the world were summoned to Rome for the funeral and to take part in the solemn meeting, the conclave, to elect the new pope. Each cardinal received this message: THE POPE IS DEAD. COME AT ONCE.

Church law mandates that the conclave must begin between the fifteenth and eighteenth day after the death of a pope. The cardinals must remain in conclave, completely shut off from the world, until the new pope is chosen.

By mid-morning, the cardinals had heard the news. It had been received in Lagos by Dominic Ekandem, the first cardinal in the history of Nigeria. It sent Brazilian Cardinal Paulo Arns, the spiritual leader of six million Catholics, into mourning. It saddened Cardinal Stephen Kim of Korea and Cardinal Terence Cooke in New York.

"So soon," cried Manila's stunned Cardinal Jaime Sin. Said Cologne's Cardinal Joseph Hoffner, "God has willed it, as painful as His will is." Boston's Cardinal Humberto Medieros declared, "I've been trying to say to God, 'It's your doing, and I must accept it.' "

In Cracow in southern Poland, Cardinal Karol Wojtyla, one of the two Polish cardinals, having said mass was having breakfast when he was told that John Paul I had died. Pushing aside his meal, he left the table and walked to his private chapel, closed the door behind him, and knelt in solitary prayer.

The bells began tolling in St. Peter's. Thousands of people, many of them red-eyed from weeping, began moving into the enormous square in front of the church to pray.

The cardinals soon began arriving in Rome for the conclave to elect the 264th successor to St. Peter. Papal elections are expensive, costing several millon dollars. Airplane fares for each of the cardinals—there were 111 cardinals at the time of John Paul's death—are the largest expense.

There is also the matter of the bonus each Vatican employee and dependent receives. Everyone, from street cleaners and dishwashers, to the editors of the official Vatican newspaper and the curators at the Vatican museum, receives $250 when a pope dies and another is elected.

7

It rained heavily on the day of the funeral. The cardinals in charge of funeral arrangements had agreed upon an open-air mass in St. Peter's Square. They decided, despite the weather, to go ahead with their plan.

The pope's body was dressed in robes of red, white, and gold, then covered with a white shroud and set on a red blanket fringed with ermine before being placed in the casket. Put with him in the coffin was a small cylindrically shaped brass case that contained a scroll certifying his death. By tradition, small sacks of gold, silver, and bronze coins and medallions bearing the pope's image and representing those that had been circulated during his reign, were also to be placed in the coffin. But John Paul I had not held office long enough for any such coins to be minted.

The coffin of plain cypress was then placed before a specially constructed altar on the rain-swept steps of St. Peter's. At one side, a tall candle flickered in the wind. A volume of the New Testament was placed on top of the coffin. It was soon soaked with rain.

By the time the funeral mass began, a crowd of about 100,000 had gathered in the square. They huddled under raincoats and umbrellas. Cardinal Confalonieri, sheltered by a canopy, recited the mass.

At the end of the ceremony, the twelve pall bearers lifted the coffin and carried it inside St. Peter's. The coffin was sealed in a lead casket, then placed in one made of oak, and finally laid to rest in a crypt beneath the main floor of the church, between crypts containing the coffins of Pope John's two namesakes, John XXIII and Paul VI.

Eight other traditional masses for the pope were held before the conclave began. At the same time, the cardinals were holding daily meetings to discuss John Paul's successor.

Officially, any baptized male Catholic in the world can be elected pope. But, since the fourteenth century, the pope had always been chosen from among the cardinals. In addition, almost all the cardinals who had become pope had been Italians. There had not been a non-Italian since 1523, the year that marked the death of Pope Adrian VI, a Dutchman.

This was partly because the pope, aside from his worldwide responsibilities, is also the Bishop of Rome. Like any bishop, he serves as the spiritual leader of his diocese, or church district, and the various parishes into which the diocese is divided.

There was also the matter of international politics. The cardinals were wary about selecting an American pope, a choice that would be likely to deepen the gulf between Western countries and those of the Eastern bloc. A candidate from a Communist country would never be considered because it would be seen as a hostile challenge to western governments. A Latin American choice might not understand the problems of the Far East or Africa. The presence of a German on the throne of St. Peter might rekindle some of the animosities of those who had suffered during World War II. An Italian was always the "safe" choice.

In the days before the conclave, newspaper reporters and television newscasters speculated on the name of the cardinal who might be elected. Cardinals Corrado Ursi of Naples, Salvatore Pappalardo of Sicily, Genoa's Giuseppe Siri, and Giovanni Benelli of Florence were among the media favorites. Cardinal Benelli had been an assistant to Pope Paul VI, whose reign had preceded that of John Paul I, and was known to be highly influential in Vatican affairs.

On the day the conclave opened, the cardinals attended a mass of the Holy Ghost and asked for spiritual guidance in the task that lay before them. They then took oaths of secrecy, each promising not to reveal the details of the balloting.

The next morning the cardinals filed into the Sistine Chapel. Twelve wooden tables had been set up beneath the magnificence of Michelangelo's famous paintings. The cardinals took their seats at the tables. All outsiders were asked to leave. The doors of the Sistine Chapel were locked.

9

The balloting began.

Church law dictates that the balloting must continue until one man receives two thirds of the votes plus one. In 1978, with 111 cardinals taking part, that meant that 75 votes were needed for election.

Following death of John Paul I, cardinals convene in the Sistine Chapel to elect a new pope. (United Press International)

Each cardinal, in keeping with tradition, filled out his ballot, a two-inch square of white paper, in disguised handwriting and carefully folded it. He then walked to the altar at one end of the chapel and prayed. He dropped his ballot into a large gold cup that had been placed on a table in front of the altar. After all the cardinals had voted, the ballots were checked and counted and the results announced.

Genoa's Cardinal Siri, with twenty-three votes, showed the most strength on the first ballot. Cardinal Benelli received twenty-two votes.

The cardinals voted a second time. Cardinal Benelli gained. But the forty votes he received were still thirty-five votes short of the seventy-five needed for election.

Outside in St. Peter's Square thousands had gathered. Every eye was focused on a makeshift stovepipe chimney on the roof of the Sistine Chapel. When the second ballot failed to elect a pope, the ballots were burned with a chemical pellet that produced black smoke, a signal to the crowd that a pope had not yet been chosen. (Before the pellet, wet straw had been burned to produce the black smoke.) Should the voting be successful, the ballots would be burned alone, and the smoke would be white. Then the crowd would break into cheers, and cries of *"Viva il papa"* ("Long live the Pope") would ring out.

In the next round of voting, Benelli's total climbed to sixty-five, only ten short of victory. To the surprise of many cardinals, Cardinal Karol Wojtyla of Poland received twenty-four votes on the third ballot. So ended the first day of the conclave.

Benelli's total increased to seventy votes on the first ballot the next day. Wojtyla received forty votes.

A fifth ballot was taken after a break for coffee. Eleven cardinals switched their votes from Benelli to Wojtyla. The tally now showed Benelli with fifty-nine, Wojtyla with fifty-one. The crowd in St. Peter's Square groaned when black smoke again puffed from the chimney.

The first ballot that afternoon produced even greater

11

strength for Wojtyla. He received seventy-three votes. Benelli's total dropped to thirty-eight.

On the eighth and final ballot, Wojtyla received ninety-seven votes. Thunderous applause filled the Sistine Chapel.

Cardinal Wojtyla, sitting alone beneath Michelangelo's "Last Judgment," bowed his head and wept.

Cardinal Villot approached Wojtyla and asked him in Latin, "Do you, Most Reverend Lord Cardinal, accept your election as Supreme Pontiff?"

There was a long pause, and then Wojtyla replied, "With obedience in faith to Christ, my Lord, and with trust in the Mother of Christ and of the church, I accept." With these words Cardinal Wojtyla became the Bishop of Rome, Vicar of Jesus Christ, Successor of the Prince of the Apostles, Supreme Pontiff of the Universal Church, Patriarch of the West, Primate of Italy, Archbishop and Metropolitan of the Rome Province, and Sovereign of the State of Vatican City.

Cardinal Villot then asked the new pope, "By what name will you be known?"

Karol Wojtyla announced his decision. He would be known as John Paul II.

After praying, the pope changed into his vestments. He donned the white silk cassock, white stockings, red velvet slippers with a small gold cross embroidered on each, white silk sash, a stole embroidered in gold, and a white silk skull cap. He was given the gold papal cross to wear, said to contain a relic of the True Cross, the cross upon which Jesus Christ was crucified. He then blessed the kneeling cardinals from whose ranks he had just stepped.

In St. Peter's Square the crowd gazed toward the chimney, tense and filled with excitement. When the first wisps of white smoke billowed from the stack, the crowd cheered and shouted. Thousands more began running toward the square as the word spread, snarling the traffic in every street in Rome west of the Tiber River.

There was now a flurry of activity inside the Vatican

Palace. Lights were switched on. The huge tapestry bearing the papal coat of arms was unrolled from the central balcony overlooking the square. Papal assistants emerged, waved, and departed.

Then the figure of Cardinal Pericle Felici appeared on the balcony. He stood in the glare of television lights, facing the crowd that had grown to well over 100,000 and was waiting expectantly for his announcement.

"I announce to you a great joy," Cardinal Felici said, speaking in Latin. "We have a new pope." The crowd roared, then quieted to hear the name.

Cardinal Felici drew out the syllables carefully. "Ca-ro-lum Cardinale Woj-ty-la." The crowd was stunned. People asked one another, "Who's he?" Some broke into half-hearted applause, but most were silent.

Journalists in the square heard a wide variety of comments.

"It's a foreign pope."

"My God, he's a Pole!"

"How do you pronounce his name?"

The crowd sent up a loud cheer when the stocky figure of John Paul II appeared on the balcony. Cardinals were on either side of him. He squinted slightly from the glare of the television lights and lifted his arms in a gesture of greeting. Then in a strong voice he gave his first blessing.

"All honor to Jesus Christ," he declared.

"Now and forever," the crowd responded.

He then delivered a short speech. The words were confident, delivered in flawlessly accented Italian. The crowd was thrilled that he could address them in their own tongue.

The pope said, "We are all still plunged in grief at the death of our beloved father, Pope John Paul I."

The crowd cheered and applauded at the mention of the previous pope's name.

"And now the Most Eminent Cardinals have chosen a

13

An estimated 300,000 people crowd St. Peter's Square for the ceremonies in which John Paul II was installed as pope. (United Press International)

new Bishop of Rome."

Another wave of applause.

"They have called me from a faraway country, but one which has always been close to the community of Christian faith and tradition."

Still more applause.

"I was afraid to accept this choice, but I did so in a spirit of humility and obedience to our Lord and complete trust in his most holy mother, the Madonna."

After another outburst the pope continued, "I do not know whether I can express myself properly in your—in *our* —Italian language. If I make mistakes, please correct me."

Shouts of "Yes, we will!" rang out.

Then the pope concluded his remarks. "Today I stand before you to make a profession of our common faith, our hope and trust in the mother of Christ and the mother of the church, and to set out on a fresh stage of the history of the church, with God's help and that of men and women."

The pope then blessed the crowd, waved, and withdrew from the balcony.

A new era had begun. Karol Wojtyla (pronounced voy-*tee*-wuh) was the first pope from Poland, the first from Eastern Europe in fact, and the first from a country dominated by a Communist government. At fifty-eight, he was the youngest pope since 1846. In robust health, it seemed possible that he could lead the Catholic Church into the twenty-first century.

He was a man of humble origins and a former factory worker. He sang and played the guitar. He skied, he hiked, he swam. He was a respected poet and playwright. He was well educated and spoke seven languages. But the most striking thing about him was that he was a Pole. He had deep feelings for Poland and the Polish Catholic Church.

He had spent his first thirty years as a priest ministering to the special needs of the Polish people. He had thus experienced life in ways unknown to most modern clergymen.

15

At 58, John Paul II was the youngest pope since 1846.
(Chris Sheridan)

During World War II, as a member of the anti-Nazi underground, he had worked to save Jewish families from the Holocaust. In more recent times, he had stood firm in the bitter struggle of his church versus Communism, the confrontation of the Gospel versus the anti-Gospel.

At a time when Christianity was crumbling in Western Europe, Karol Wojtyla saw it flourish in Eastern Europe. At a time when policies of Western nations had seemed inadequate in coping with Communist expansion, he demonstrated true deftness in dealing with the Communist mind. He had spoken out on poverty, sex and marriage, and human rights. Now he loomed as the most important leader of the Catholic Church in this century.

CHAPTER

2

"IF YOU PITCH YOUR TENT IN THE MIDDLE OF FIFTH Avenue, you are going to be hit by a bus." That is how Igor Stravinsky, the great composer, once described Poland and the keystone position it occupies in central Europe.

Warring European nations have invaded and conquered Poland for centuries. The conquerers have often divided Poland among themselves, and for long periods of time the nation did not exist as a separate country.

Communist rule was thrust upon Poland after World War II. Most of the country's 36 million people, 90 percent of whom are Catholics, oppose the Communists. But anti-Communist resistance is crushed by the army, the police, or by other repressive methods.

Karol Josef Wojtyla was born in Wadowice in southern Poland on May 18, 1920, in the shadow of the 600-year-old Cathedral of St. Mary. Karol is Polish for Charles.

Wadowice is a small farm town not far from the Carpathian Mountains that form Poland's southern border with Czechoslovakia. It is also a market town where country people bring their produce—beets, potatoes, and wheat—to sell.

Just a year before Karol was born, Poland had become a free nation once more under the terms of the Treaty of Versailles, which was hammered out at the end of World War I. It had been controlled by other nations for 123 years. Large areas of land were given over to Poland from the defeated German nation. But then a boundary dispute triggered a war with Russia. The Treaty of Riga in 1921 brought peace again and established Poland's eastern border.

Karol was named for his father, a lieutenant in the Polish Army assigned to the Regional Draft Board in Wadowice. A dark-haired, good-looking man with a mustache and glasses, he was a stern disciplinarian. Karol's mother, Emilia, a pretty round-faced woman, had once been a school teacher.

The family included one other child, Edward, who was fifteen when Karol was born. At the time of Karol's birth, Edward was studying to be a doctor.

Little is known of Karol's childhood. He entered grade school in Wadowice in 1927. His parents and close friends called him Lolek, an often-used nickname for Karol. A photograph from this period shows him to have a strong facial resemblance to his mother. His hair was closely cropped, a schoolboy custom of the time.

The Wojtyla family lived on the first floor of a modest apartment on Church Street in Wadowice. They were not well off, but not poor either. The Wojtylas had running water, and not all families did.

Tragedy struck the Wojtyla family when Karol was nine years old. His mother died while giving birth to a third child, a girl, who also died during the birth. With Edward away working in a hospital, Karol and his father were alone.

Karol's father loved his son, but demanded obedience. In keeping with his military training and experience, Mr.

(Neil Katine)

Wojtyla established a schedule that the nine-year-old Karol followed every day. It included early morning mass at the cathedral where Karol was an altar boy who assisted the priest. After mass, Karol went to school. When he returned home, he ate supper. Then he was permitted an hour of playtime. Karol used the time to dash off to a nearby field with a friend who lived across the street and practice kicking a soccer ball. After playing, Karol did his homework.

Life became harder for the Wojtylas. Karol's father, who had retired from the Army, found it difficult to provide for his young son on a lieutenant's pension. Then tragedy struck a second time. An epidemic of scarlet fever broke out in the hospital where Edward was working, and the disease claimed Karol's brother as one of its victims.

The death of his oldest son, for whom a bright future

21

A childhood picture of Karol Wojtyla, posing with a candle after receiving his First Communion. Close-cropped hair was a schoolboy custom of the time. (United Press International)

had been forecast, coming so soon after the death of his wife, deeply affected both Karol and his father. Karol would sometimes wander aimlessly through the streets of Wadowice, lost in his loneliness.

Karol had moved on to high school by this time. He was popular there and an excellent student. He had developed a love for Polish literature, but he was not the type of student who would spend long hours reading. There was too much else that he liked to do. He loved sports. Stocky and sturdily built, he became one of his school's best soccer players. His favorite position was goalie. He also liked swimming and going for long walks.

Young Karol felt great joy during his frequent visits to the wild and rugged Tatra Mountains, part of the Central Carpathians and not far from his home. He became skilled in mountaineering and skiing.

"Karol *belongs* with the mountain people," a friend once said of him. "He loves their songs and poetry; he shares their simplicity, their sense of humor, their independence, their love of freedom. They have always been in love with freedom. Karol has a lot of mountain man in his makeup. He, too, is in love with freedom."

Acting and the theater were among Karol's chief interests, and he took part in all of his school's plays, often being cast in one of the leading roles. He came to possess a rich baritone voice. Not only did he become skilled as an actor, but he also excelled in dancing—performing folk dances, waltzes, and the lively and difficult Polish mazurka.

Karol still served as an altar boy, and he headed a school religious society. Yet fellow students remember him not so much for his interest in religion as for his love of literature, drama, and athletics. His ambitions were linked with the theater.

"He was vivid, quick-minded and very good, by nature an optimist," one of his teachers once recalled. "He was a good schoolboy."

Just before Karol and his classmates were to take their

The Wojtyla family home in Wadowice.
(Zbigniew Putyra)

final exams, the school was visited by Bishop Adam Stefan Sapieha of Cracow. Karol, perhaps because of his excellent voice, was chosen to deliver the words of thanks to the Bishop on behalf of the students.

Bishop Sapieha was very much impressed by the young orator. "Is that boy going to become a priest?" the bishop asked of one of Karol's teachers.

"I don't believe so at the moment," the teacher replied.

"Too bad," said the bishop. "He'd make a fine one."

After graduation from high school, Karol decided to attend the famed Jagiellonian University in Cracow, about thirty-five miles from Wadowice. His father, rather than live alone, gave up the family home and went with Karol. They shared an apartment in Cracow.

Cracow is one of the world's most beautiful and historical cities. As early as the ninth century, it was one of the leading commercial centers of Europe. By the twelfth century, it had become Poland's capital. The city was captured and destroyed by invading bands of Tartars in the thirteenth century, but by the next century it had been restored to its former eminence and was as prosperous as ever. Cracow has been called a Royal City, a Holy City, and the Polish Athens. It is a treasure trove of art and architecture. It is Poland's third largest city today (after Warsaw and Lodz), with a population of about 700,000.

One of Cracow's jewels is Jagiellonian University, founded in 1364 by King Casmir the Great. It is the oldest university in central Europe. By the middle of the fifteenth century, Jagiellonian University had won wide renown for the new ideas it had developed in science and philosophy. Students from every corner of Europe went to study there. One of the most famous was Mikolaj Kopernik (Copernicus), the brilliant astronomer who developed the theory that the earth is a moving planet. Copernicus is considered to be the founder of the science of astronomy.

Karol entered the Jagiellonian University to study Pol-

Childhood scenes of Karol Wojtyla from Marvel Comics'
"The Life of Pope John Paul II," published in 1982.

ish language and literature, but much of his time and energy was devoted to the stage. He joined the student drama group and was soon performing modern plays as well as those with themes based on Polish history. One offering was *Knight of the Moon*, a drama based on an old Polish legend. Each of the actors represented a different astrological sign. Karol, being stocky and muscular, was assigned the role of Taurus the Bull. Theater posters of the day showed Karol, at nineteen, to be smiling and handsome.

Storm clouds were gathering. Adolph Hitler had come to power in Germany. Hitler's troops marched into the Rhineland in 1936, thus putting German soldiers at the French border. It was a clear violation of the Treaty of Versailles.

Hitler became bolder. In March 1938, he sent his troops into Austria. It took only a few days to bring the country under Nazi control. European leaders wrung their hands but did nothing.

Hitler eyed Czechoslovakia next, Poland's neighbor to the south. One part of Czechoslovakia—the Sudetenland—was the homeland for three and a half million German-speaking people who were not Czechs. Hitler demanded that the Czech government give up the Sudetenland to Germany. The Czech government refused. The French announced that they would stand by the Czechs, and Great Britain agreed to support the French.

All of Europe seemed poised on the brink of war. Prime Minister Neville Chamberlain of Britain, seeing himself as a peacemaker, flew to Germany to meet with Hitler. Their conversations led to the Munich Agreement. Under its terms the Czechs agreed to give up the Sudetenland to Germany. In return Hitler made a solemn pledge to Chamberlain to make no further territorial claims in Europe.

Hitler broke his promise a few months later when he ordered his troops to occupy the rest of Czechoslovakia in March 1939.

Poland loomed as the next Nazi victim. The British said they would go to war if Hitler attacked Poland, but Hitler believed they were bluffing. He felt that the British would never fight in support of the Poles unless they could enlist the support of the Russians. He decided he would beat the British to the punch. He sent top-level diplomats to Moscow to bargain with the Russian leader, Joseph Stalin.

The Russians' government was just as much a dictatorship as was the Germans'. Stalin had conducted murderous purges to liquidate anyone suspected of opposing him. He had seized private property, outlawed all political parties except the Communist Party, and had denied religious and other freedoms to the Russian people.

Hitler hated Russia, but he also feared the nation. He had denounced the country for years as Germany's deadliest enemy. But Hitler knew he needed Stalin's support. A nonaggression pact between the two countries was signed on August 23, 1939. Now Hitler no longer had to worry about Russia. The nonaggression pact with Russia made World War II a certainty, because it made him free to do as he wanted.

At dawn on September 1, 1939, German troops invaded Poland. That day is forever etched in Karol's memory. September 1 happened to be the first Friday in September. For many Catholics, the first Friday of each month is a day of special devotion to the Virgin Mary. It was for Karol. He got up early and went to Wawel Cathedral to help serve mass. While there, he heard the sirens start to wail and the bombing begin. He helped serve mass that morning to the thunder of falling bombs and the clatter of antiaircraft guns.

Karol's days became filled with fear and apprehension. Radio news bulletins reported that Hitler's armies were overrunning Poland. Hundreds of tanks and fast armored vehicles, supported by waves of screaming dive bombers, surged through the Polish lines. The Polish army was routed within a week. On September 6 Cracow fell. Karol watched as the German troops marched into the city. Warsaw fell two days later.

On September 17, with Poland ready to collapse, Russia attacked from the east. Poland surrendered on September 27. The next day, Russia and Germany divided Poland. Hitler swore, "I shall make Poland a long forgotten name on ancient maps."

A new order fell upon Poland. Hans Frank, a leading Nazi, was made Governor General. "We must annihilate the Jews," Frank declared. A "quarantine camp," as the Nazis called it, was established at Auschwitz, not far from Cracow. It was to become one of the most notorious of all the Nazi concentration camps.

Karol had been getting ready for his second year at college. But there was to be no studying for him or for anyone else. The Germans closed Jagiellonian University not long after they arrived in Cracow. Early in November the Germans called a meeting of the teaching staff. Many professors believed it was being held to discuss the reopening of the University. But the meeting was a trap. The professors who attended were taken to concentration camps.

It was just as perilous to be a student as it was to be a professor. Many of Karol's friends had already been arrested and taken to concentration camps or sent to Germany as forced labor. "The Poles," Hans Frank said on taking office, "shall be the slaves of the German Reich." The Germans began issuing work cards. Any Pole caught without one was likely to end up in a slave labor camp in Germany, which, in the eyes of the Germans, was a most appropriate place for the Poles.

It was obvious to Karol that he had to do what everyone else was doing. He obtained a work card. Not long after, he began toiling away in a limestone quarry on the outskirts of Cracow. Both summer and winter the air was filled with choking dust. The constant noise of steel drills and hammers assaulted the workers' ears.

Karol and other young men newly assigned to the quarry were given the job of shoveling up stone debris after a section of the quarry wall had been blasted. And when sections of the quarry flooded, they were made to pump out the water with old, hand-operated pumps. Karol's body ached in a hundred places at the end of each working day.

Later, Karol operated a pneumatic hammer, crushing big chunks of stone into pieces of usable size. The trick was to wield the hammer in such a way that the rock would shatter as quickly as possible. Injury to the eyes or face from flying pieces of stone was a constant hazard.

Still later, Karol was made an assistant to the man in charge of dynamiting operations. Karol would place the explosive charge and fuse in the drilled hole. His boss would light the fuse. Then they would both run. Other workers would attack the big chunks of rocks with their hammers once the dust had settled.

Karol worked in the quarry for almost two years. This period made a deep impression on him. He later wrote a poem called "The Quarry." Published in 1957, it described quarry life in stark detail:

> *Hands are the heart's landscape. They split*
>   *sometimes*
> *like ravines into which an undefined force rolls*
> *The very same hands which man only opens*
> *when his palms have had their fill of toil*
> *Now he sees: because of him alone others can*
>   *walk in peace*

The poem was dedicated to a fellow worker who had been killed. "A stone smashed his temples," says the poem, "and cut through his heart's chamber." It concludes:

> *Should his anger now flow into the anger of others?*
> *It was maturing in him through its own truth*
>   *and love,*
> *Should he be used by those that come after,*
>   *deprived*
> *of substance, unique and deeply his own?*

Karol's workday at the quarry began early in the morning and ended at mid-afternoon. The little money he earned was the only income he and his father now had, since his father's pension had stopped with the war's outbreak.

Karol never stopped being a student during the war. Higher education simply went underground. Throughout Cracow and other university cities, students held secret classes at night in private homes, apartments, churches, and shops.

Karol was also active in an underground theater group, the Rhapsodic Theater, during the first years of the war. Some sources say that he founded the group. It staged performances in cellars or private homes. Karol and the others would recite poetry or perform dramatic works for audiences of from fifteen to twenty. The poetry and plays never failed to stress Polish culture and history.

Karol also worked with a Polish resistance movement, the Home Army. The Army was in charge of helping escapees, collecting military information, and distributing resistance literature. Karol would take Jewish families out of their ghettos, find them hiding places, and obtain new identities for them. He saved many families from death. He lived in daily danger of losing his life.

The resistance group to which Karol belonged obtained important information for the Allies about Nazi experiments with the V-1 and V-2 missiles. The Germans were testing these missiles in Poland.

Suffering and tragedy were everywhere. Children were snatched from their parents and deported. Jewish families were rounded up, beaten, and sent to concentration camps. There were daily shootings in the streets. There was the constant fear of the knock on the door in the middle of the night, of being dragged off to prison or sent to Auschwitz. At night, after curfew hours, when no one was supposed to walk the streets, the police would suddenly appear in numbers to rope off an entire block. They would arrest or shoot anyone trapped in their net.

From time to time, rumors were heard of the horrors unfolding at Auschwitz. The stories were so monstrous that they seemed beyond belief.

31

CHAPTER

3

AT SOME TIME IN 1942, DURING THE DARKEST DAYS of the war, Karol Wojtyla decided to become a priest. The suffering and misery all around him may have been a spur in making his decision. In addition, his own life had been touched by tragedy. His father had died of heart failure during the first year of the war, and Karol had spent twelve hours in prayer at his deathbed. They had become very close in the last year of Karol's father's life. Now Karol was alone in the world.

Karol himself had a brush with death during this time. He was knocked down by a tram as he was crossing a street in Cracow and suffered a fractured skull. He spent weeks recovering. Only a few months later, he was struck by a truck carrying German soldiers and narrowly escaped death. Injuries he received in the second accident gave him a permanent stoop.

Karol's decision to become a priest was also influenced

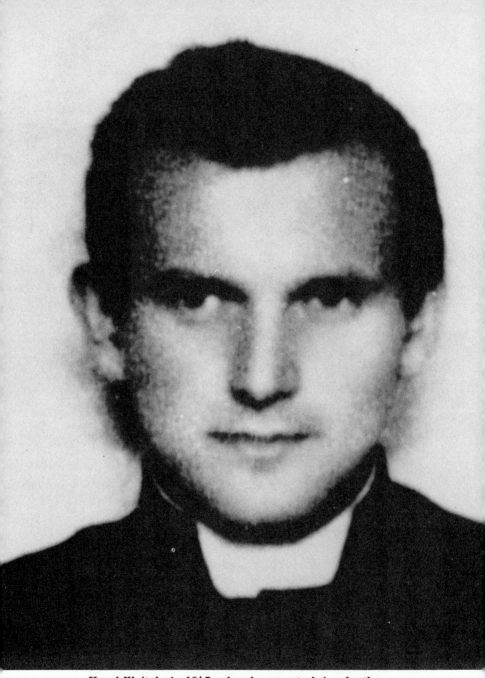

Karol Wojtyla in 1945, when he was studying for the priesthood. (United Press International)

by Jan Tyranowski, a tailor in Cracow about twice Karol's age. Tyranowski organized groups of young people who would meet frequently to recite the rosary, a series of prayers in devotion to the Virgin Mary.

Tyranowski sought to show Karol and the other members of the prayer group how to live, not merely close to God, but how to develop a fellowship with God, to live with God inside themselves. He recommended to Karol that he study and seek to imitate the life of St. John of the Cross, a sixteenth-century Spanish monk, poet, and mystic. It has been said that the works of St. John of the Cross can only be practiced and understood by someone who has received the gift of mystical prayer. Tyranowski believed that Karol possessed that unusual gift.

Karol presented himself to a priest at the Wawel Cathedral and announced that he wanted to become a priest. The Nazis had forbidden studying for the priesthood. The reason for that policy was not difficult to understand. The Nazis knew that in order to destroy Poland they would first have to destroy its Catholic Church because it played such a vital role in the nation's life and culture.

But the seminaries, the special schools where young men were educated for the priesthood, had, like so much else in Poland, gone underground. Most of the students lived in the country, serving as assistants to parish priests and studying on their own under the direction of Archbishop Sapieha and members of his staff. Karol, although he had been accepted as a candidate for the priesthood, continued to go to his job each day. He had been transferred from the quarry to a chemical factory, where he tended the boilers that provided the factory's heat and hot water. He spent every spare moment reading or studying.

In addition to his studies and his job at the chemical plant, Karol continued to work with the resistance movement. He was also involved in another secret organization, through which students helped one another find food and shelter. His life followed this perilous path from 1942 to 1944.

By the summer of 1944 the German war machine was showing signs of collapse. From bases in North Africa, the Allies had stormed into Sicily and then invaded Italy. On June 6, 1944, D-Day, Allied forces had landed in Normandy and had begun the long advance through France toward Germany's heartland. Allied bombers were blasting German industrial centers every night.

Meanwhile, Soviet forces were pressuring the Germans from the east. (Hitler, not trusting his one-time partner, Stalin, had invaded Russia in 1941.) The Russians recaptured the Ukraine, much of Lithuania, and swept into eastern Poland. By the end of July, the Soviet Army was only forty miles from Warsaw.

The Poles of Warsaw, believing that they would soon be supported by the Russian allies, rose up against their German conquerers on August 1, 1944. The whole nation was thrilled by their courage. In the first few days of the uprising they gained control of many sections of the city. But their lack of food and ammunition ultimately forced the Poles to surrender. Hitler, in a vengeful mood, ordered the destruction of Warsaw's historical and cultural monuments. More than 200,000 Polish citizens lost their lives during the revolt. Meanwhile, the Soviet Army halted its advance at the gates of Warsaw. They stood by and did nothing to aid the valiant Polish people.

The enraged Germans sought vengeance in other parts of Poland. In Cracow they smashed in the doors of homes and dragged the occupants into the streets. Some Poles were murdered in public. All able-bodied men were rounded up, thrust into police cars, and taken off.

Miraculously, the German troops never entered Karol's house at 10 Tyniecka Street even though the door was not locked. Karol was inside kneeling in prayer, unaware that a roundup was taking place.

Afterward, Archbishop Sapieha decided to act. Fearing for the lives of the handful of young men who were studying for the priesthood, he made plans to place them under his protection. He sent a messenger to Karol and the others telling them to bring their belongings and come immediately to live within the walls of the palace. There they could continue their studies for the priesthood.

Once Karol had begun to live at the Archbishop's Palace, the Germans quickly detected his absence from the chemical plant. His name was added to the absent workers' list, and the police began an active search for him.

Archbishop Sapieha was a remarkable man. He treated the German occupiers of his city with contempt. The people of Cracow loved him. The Germans, although they probably had the archbishop marked for execution, treated him with respect. Hans Frank, the Governor General, would sometimes pay the archbishop a visit. When he did, his host would serve the German leader thin slices of black bread with beetroot preserve and coffee made from grain—the same food that the Poles were eating. The last time the Governor General called upon the cardinal he did not suspect that there were several young students hidden in the building, one of whom was Karol Wojtyla.

The students lived together in a large room that had been converted into a dormitory. The furniture consisted of their metal beds and a few chairs. A big table in the center of the room was used for reading and writing. Their meals were sent to them on trays. The students seldom stepped outside.

Archbishop Sapieha furnished each of the students with a cassock, the long black garment that reaches to the feet, traditionally worn by members of the clergy. The cassocks made the students look like priests. If any German soldiers happened to enter the palace grounds and spot them, they would be safer than had they been wearing ordinary clothes. The students were also furnished with fake identity cards.

A daily routine in the palace was soon established. The students would arise at six, meditate in the chapel, then attend a mass offered by the archbishop. Two of the students would act as servers. Breakfast was next; then studies began. The main meal was served at noon. The afternoon and evening were taken up with private studies and prayer services in the chapel.

As the Russian troops grew closer, Soviet planes began to raid Cracow. The Germans answered with antiaircraft fire. By this time, January 1945, the Nazis had scarcely any planes to send into the sky against the Russians.

Russian bombers shattered the palace windows and blasted tiles from the roof. During the raids the students took shelter in an underground room where they prayed and sang hymns.

One January night when the students were huddled in the underground shelter, the first of the Russian soldiers entered. The students realized immediately that the Germans had fled Cracow and that the occupation was over. They served the Russians tea and bread, which was all they had.

Cracow had emerged from the war relatively unharmed, at least when compared to Warsaw. The Polish capital suffered greater damage than Berlin, the target of constant Allied bombing raids of massive proportions.

The Catholic Church had been subjected to an unrelenting reign of terror during the war. A total of 3,646 priests had been imprisoned in concentration camps; of that number, 2,647 were murdered.

For the Polish nation as a whole, the war was a terrible catastrophe. More than six million Polish citizens died during the six years of Nazi occupation, three million of whom were Jews. In other words, one Pole out of every four had been killed.

The horror of Nazi rule was revealed at Auschwitz. When the first Soviet troops entered the camp, they found human ashes and charred bones scattered everywhere. Huge piles of human hair were found in storerooms. Later, the International Military Tribunal in Nuremberg would announce that four million people had perished at Auschwitz.

Once the war was over, Karol and his classmates were able to come out of hiding and continue their studies openly. They began attending classes at the Theological Seminary, a part of the Jagiellonian University. Eventually they began living there.

Classmates of Karol's during this period remember him as a diligent student who read constantly. He always had a book in his hands. His holiness was apparent. He would head every page of notes with such initials as "J + M" (for Jesus and Mary) or "AMDG" (Ad majorem Dei gloriam—To the greater glory of God).

Soviet soldiers continued to occupy Poland. One day Karol had an unusual encounter with one of them. Karol was at the seminary where he lived when the doorbell rang. When Karol opened the door, a young Russian soldier was standing there.

"What do you want?" Karol asked.

"I want to enter the seminary," the soldier replied. "I want to become a priest."

Karol could hardly believe his ears. Such a request from a Soviet soldier seemed incredible to him. Karol invited the young man into the seminary, and they talked for hours.

Later, Karol spoke of the incident. "The young man had scarcely even been inside a church. At school and later at work he had continuously been assured, 'There is no God.' In spite of everything, the young soldier kept on saying that God did exist."

The incident made a deep impression on young Karol. He would never forget its significance.

During this period Karol became deeply involved with a student self-help organization. Many of his fellow students lived under wretched conditions. Their parents had been lost or murdered during the war. They dressed in rags, lived in cellars or shanties, and seemed on the brink of starvation. UNRRA (the United Nations Relief and Rehabilitation Administration) had been sending food and clothing to Poland, and one of the duties of the organization to which

39

Karol belonged was to distribute the parcels to those in the greatest need.

Karol's student days in Cracow were drawing to a close. He was ordained as a priest in Archbishop Sapieha's chapel on November 1, 1946. He was twenty-six years old. The next day, All Souls Day, an important feast day in Poland, Father Wojtyla said his first mass at St. Leonard's Chapel in Cracow's Wawel Cathedral.

After he had offered mass the following Sunday, a family friend held a small reception in his honor. All of his closest friends attended. There were speeches in his honor and much good feeling and laughter. But there was a touch of sadness, too. Archbishop Sapieha (soon to be made a cardinal) was sending his newly ordained priest to Rome to study for two years. It was obvious from his decision that the archbishop recognized that Karol was a young man of more than ordinary talents who should be permitted the enrichment of additional study. While his friends congratulated Karol on his good fortune, they were not happy to see him leave Cracow.

Karol worked toward a doctorate in philosophy at Angelicum University in Rome. In order to earn such a degree, a student must complete a lengthy paper, or thesis, that involves much original research. Karol's thesis concerned St. John of the Cross, the Spanish poet and mystic.

Karol learned to speak Italian while living in Rome. And when he went to France during his summer vacation in 1947, he worked to improve his French.

Karol's friends in Cracow received lengthy letters from him. His studies delighted him, he reported, although they kept him very busy. "Each day is absolutely packed," he wrote.

"I am always in spiritual touch with Poland," he said in another letter. "I am always thinking about my country. I pray for her. . . ."

CHAPTER

4

WHEN KAROL WOJTYLA RETURNED TO POLAND IN 1948, ready to take up his first assignment as a parish priest, he found a country vastly different from the one he had left. The government was in the hands of the Communists and was preparing for open warfare on the Catholic Church.

Poland's fate after World War II had been sealed by the terms of the Yalta Conference, held early in 1945 when Germany's collapse was apparent. President Franklin Roosevelt of the United States, Prime Minister Winston Churchill of Great Britain, and Russian Premier Joseph Stalin attended the conference. Under the terms of the agreement they reached, about one-third of prewar Poland was given to Russia. Poland was to be compensated by being given certain German territories. The Yalta Conference has been severely criticized for its "betrayal" of Poland.

The Yalta Agreement also provided for free elections in

Poland and other liberated nations. Poland did have elections, but they were anything but "free." In 1947, candidates of parties other than the Communist Party were beaten up or shot. Their campaign literature was destroyed. No one was surprised when the Soviet-supported candidates won in every district.

Poland became a "People's Republic." Soviet "advisors" were in control. Red flags and portraits of Stalin and Lenin were everywhere.

The people of Poland soon found that they were subjected to a type of slavery. They were not the personal property of a master, but their conditions were not much different from that. They had no legal rights against the state. As workers, their wages and terms of employment were dictated. For trying to escape they could be imprisoned or even shot.

The new government was afraid of the Catholic Church and had begun a crackdown similar to that under Nazi rule. Schools all over the country were taken over by the government. Religious education in schools was now forbidden. Catholic newspapers were heavily censored, and public meetings of a religious nature were prohibited. By the end of 1948, some 400 priests were either in prisons or concentration camps.

It was against this background of tension and strife that Father Wojtyla began his career as a parish priest. He was assigned to a small parish in the village of Niegowic, not far from Cracow. Karol's duties were to assist the pastor, the priest in charge of the parish.

The parish was located in a remote area. The house in which the priests lived had no electricity, and water came from a well. There was a garden, an orchard, chickens, and cows.

Karol's friends found it hard to understand why he was being sent to such a remote place. Years of difficult study in Rome seemed hardly necessary for a parish priest in Niegowic.

Karol saw nothing wrong with his assignment, however. He scoffed at those who suggested he should be involved in more important duties. Being a parish priest *was* important, he felt, and he took up his new duties eagerly.

The day began with mass, after which he taught classes in Christian doctrine to local school children or called upon the sick and elderly of the parish, those too feeble to attend religious services at the church. On Sunday he preached. The people flocked to hear him.

As a priest, Karol was now empowered to hear confessions and administer the sacrament of penance. Catholics believe that when they confess their sins to a priest, expressing sincere sorrow for having sinned, and promising to try not to sin in the future, the priest can forgive their sins in God's name. This is the Sacrament of Penance. The effect of penance is to reconcile a person to God and the Christian community.

Hour after hour, Karol would sit in the confessional of the parish church. People of the parish would enter, kneel, bless themselves, and then acknowledge their sins to him. Father Wojtyla would listen, impart advice, and assign each person a penance to perform. The penance usually took the form of prayers to be said.

To Father Wojtyla, no priestly duty was more important than hearing confessions. "It is there," he once said, "that one encounters human beings at the depth of their personality."

Father Wojtyla remained at Niegowic for about a year. The villagers there remember him fondly. "It was too good to last," one of them once recalled. "The very first day we saw him, we knew they'd soon take him from us."

Father Wojtyla was next assigned to the much larger and busier parish of St. Florian's in Cracow. He arrived in a rickety, old horse-drawn cart, carrying only a small suitcase and a few books.

One of the men of the parish climbed into the cart and began to look for Father Wojtyla's suitcase. "Your luggage, Father," he asked. "Where is your luggage?"

"Luggage?" he replied. "What luggage?" And he held up his small suitcase.

The parishioners of St. Florian's soon realized that material possessions did not interest their new priest. Many considered the cassock he wore to be disgraceful. It was worn and patched, and new patches kept appearing regularly. Even on the coldest days, he would wear the cassock and nothing else, not even a sweater, to protect himself from the freezing temperatures. He would sit by the hour in the confessional on the coldest days in the heatless church. The parishioners began to fear that he was going to freeze to death. They took up a collection and bought him a new cassock and a fine overcoat. Father Wojtyla accepted the cassock, but the parishioners never saw him wear the overcoat. They decided that he must have given it away.

When parishioners went to St. Florian's and asked for Father Wojtyla they were usually told, "Try the confessional; he's probably there." And it was in the confessional that he was usually to be found. He was not necessarily hearing confessions. He used the confessional for praying, meditating, or reading.

The people soon began to understand that Father Wojtyla was "different." The housekeeper who cleaned his room noticed that his bed was seldom slept in. He either slept on the floor or worked or prayed through the night.

Father Wojtyla was put in charge of the altar boys at St. Florian's, instructing them and supervising them in their duties. It was a task he took very seriously. He would often visit the boys in their homes, not to offer advice or instruction, but simply to chat with them and their parents.

Father Wojtyla also became popular with groups of students from Jagiellonian University. He frequently went on weekend outings with them—hiking, biking, or skiing in the Beskid Mountains, or canoeing on the Brdza or Czarna Hancza Rivers. These were fun-filled expeditions. His young companions called Father Wojtyla "wujek," which

44

means "little uncle." They would laugh and joke together, sing and pray, and roast potatoes on open fires. And Karol would offer mass each day. He and the students would discuss God, themselves, the world, and Poland's past and future.

"We called him the eternal teen-ager," a friend recalls. "When he was with young people, he relived his own student days."

Father Wojtyla became enormously popular at St. Florian's. In Poland, as in many other Catholic countries, it is the custom to celebrate a person's "name day," the day of the saint after whom the person is named, rather than the person's birthday. When the feast of St. Charles arrived, it seemed as if every man, woman, and child in the parish stopped at the priest's house to shake Karol's hand and wish him well.

Father Wojtyla's reputation was beginning to spread beyond the parish boundaries of St. Florian's. On Sundays when he preached, men and women came from all parts of Cracow to listen. "You could sense that he longed to take you by the hand and lead you to God," one of his parishioners recalls.

During this period Karol was writing poetry. One day he brought a collection of his poems to Jerzy Turowicz, the editor of one of Poland's leading Catholic weekly newspapers, and asked him if he would be interested in publishing some of them. Turowicz liked the poems. They were religious in nature, intelligent, and thought provoking. Karol asked that the poems be published under the name of Andrzej Jawien.

Karol continued to write poetry in the years that followed. (Poems of his were published as late as 1975.) His work became stronger and more philosophical and often took the form of religious reflections within a poetic structure.

In a poem called "The Negro," Karol expressed a unity

of spirit with people of distant lands:

> *My dear brother, it's you, an immense land I feel*
> *where rivers dry up suddenly—and the sun burns*
> *the body as the furnace burns ore*
> *I feel your thoughts like mine.*

In another poem, titled "The Marble Floor," Karol addressed St. Peter directly:

> *Peter, you are the floor, that others*
> *may walk over you (not knowing*
> *where they go), you guide their steps . . .*
> *The rock is a gigantic temple floor,*
> *the cross a pasture.*

For a period of three years during the late 1950s, no poems of Karol's were published. But in December 1960, the name Andrzej Jawien appeared again as the author of a play, *The Goldsmith's Shop*. It was a play largely made up of monologues delivered by people who spoke not directly to one another but to the audience. In the play, subtitled *Meditations on the Sacrament of Marriage*, the leading characters reflect on the development and changing nature of their love for one another.

At the time he had taken on his assignment at St. Florian's, Father Wojtyla had also resumed classes at the Jagiellonian University, studying ethics—the rules of human conduct and the system of moral principles. But he was so smothered by his work and other activities at St. Florian's that he did not have enough time to study.

In the midst of this dilemma, Cardinal Sapieha died. It was a heavy blow to Father Wojtyla. The Cardinal, as the archbishop of Cracow, had shepherded Karol's education and sponsored his study in Rome. Cardinal Sapieha had opposed the Stalinist regime with just as much fervor as he had struggled against Hitler and the Nazis. The people of Cracow called him their "invincible cardinal."

The Soviets stepped up their campaign to downgrade

the Catholic Church. Large gatherings were now forbidden. But at Cardinal Sapieha's funeral, when huge, weeping crowds filled the streets of Cracow, the police were scarcely seen. They realized that by refusing to permit the outpouring of grief, they could easily have triggered a general uprising.

The procession bearing the cardinal's body wound its way through the city to Wawel Cathedral for burial. Father Wojtyla was one of the priests who helped carry the coffin.

Not long after Cardinal Sapieha's death in 1951, his successor, Archbishop Eugeniusz Baziak, spoke to Karol and advised him to give up pastoral work if he expected to make any real advancement in his education. The archbishop would not agree to any "half-and-half solutions," Father Wojtyla told a friend. So Karol relinquished his duties as a parish priest and resumed studying on a full-time basis at Jagiellonian University. In two years' time, he had earned a second doctorate.

These were troubled times for the Catholic Church in Poland. Seminaries were being closed throughout the country and their students sent to labor camps. By the end of 1952, over nine hundred priests and eight bishops were in prison. Archbishop Baziak, Father Wojtyla's superior, was among those jailed.

Relations between the Communist regime and the church reached their lowest ebb in 1953 when Cardinal Wyszynski, the leader of the Catholic Church in Poland, was placed under house arrest in an isolated monastery in the southern part of the country.

It was not merely the Catholic Church that was oppressed. Stalin's secret police were everywhere, and arrests were a common occurrence. Hundreds of people were liquidated, including many who had fought bravely against the Germans during World War II.

Father Wojtyla remained in the background during this period of strife, concentrating on teaching and writing. He was invited to lecture at the Catholic University of Lublin.

In Eastern Poland, a bit more than 100 miles from the Russian border, the Catholic University of Lublin was the only university not controlled by the state. Father Wojtyla made an excellent impression with his lecturing, and he was invited to become a member of the university faculty. In 1955 he was named to head the university's ethics department.

Whenever he spoke, Father Wojtyla drew large crowds. "He was not a dry theoretician," one student recalls, "but was always showing problems in the context of life's experiences. In him, theory and practice melted together."

The death of Joseph Stalin in 1953 marked the beginning of a thaw in relations between the Polish and the Soviet regime. But the easing of tensions did not happen overnight, and only after there were bloody workers' riots in Poznan and other cities.

On August 15, 1956, the Feast of the Assumption, a holy day on the Catholic calendar that marks the bodily taking up into heaven of the Virgin Mary, one and one-half million people converged on the hilltop monastery of Our Lady of Czestochowa, not far from Cracow, to call for an end to Soviet oppression and to ask for the release of Cardinal Wyszynski, who was still under house arrest. They carried the cardinal's empty throne, upon which had been placed a giant spray of red and white roses (red and white are the national colors of Poland).

During October of that year, Wladyslaw Gomulka, long a Polish political leader, became head of Poland's Communist Party and immediately began relaxing the government's campaign against religion. Cardinal Wyszynski was released from prison, as were many priests and bishops. Religious instruction was again permitted in the schools. Freedom and tolerance became the order of the day. The Catholic Church, for its part, had to recognize the existing political situation and encourage the citizenry to work "for the good of the country."

It was during this period of relative harmony (which lasted only a few years) that Father Wojtyla was made a bishop. The appointment came in 1958.

At the time, Father Wojtyla held no special office within the church. And he was, at thirty-eight, relatively young. (He would be the youngest Polish bishop.) So the appointment was quite unexpected.

Father Wojtyla was on a canoeing expedition with a group of friends when the news was brought to him. He returned with the messenger to Warsaw to meet with Cardinal Wyszynski. "The Pope has nominated you to become a bishop," the cardinal said. "Will you accept?"

Father Wojtyla was silent for a moment. Then he asked if he could wait until he had finished his canoe trip. The cardinal agreed. Father Wojtyla enjoyed a few more days of relaxation. When he returned to Cracow, the announcement was made.

CHAPTER
5

BECOMING A BISHOP DID NOTHING TO CHANGE KAROL
Wojtyla's life-style. He still lived in a small, one-bedroom
apartment in Cracow. His favorite means of transportation
had long been the bicycle, and it continued to be. He still
wore a threadbare cassock and shoes with worn-down
heels.

His burden of work so increased that it became difficult
for him to get to Lublin to teach, so his students came to
him, traveling the 110 miles from Lublin to Cracow. His
seminars were held in an old, crumbling building not far
from Wawel Cathedral. They would begin during the afternoon and often last until midnight, whereupon the students
would then make the journey back to Lublin by bus or train.

He did not want his being a bishop to isolate him from
his people, so he began the practice of holding "oplatek"
get-togethers. The oplatek is a white, circular wafer of un-
leavened bread, imprinted with a Biblical scene such as the

birth of Jesus or the Last Supper, which Poles traditionally break into pieces on Christmas Eve and share with one another as a sign of love.

Bishop Wojtyla would break oplatek wafers at the students' church of St. Anne's, and everyone in the church would share in the pieces as a sign of unity. The practice quickly spread to other churches.

Then Bishop Wojtyla began having oplatek gatherings in his home. At least once a week he would invite groups of doctors, artists, scientists, lawyers, students, or clerks, both Catholics and non-Catholics, to his cramped apartment. The table would be festively set—but with no food. Those attending were invited to have a glass of wine and share the oplatek wafer. The evening would often end with music and the singing of hymns.

Sometimes Bishop Wojtyla took groups of his students on treks deep into the Wolski woods near Cracow or on long expeditions into the Tatra Mountains. The bishop would sit on a log or a big rock and lecture to the students sprawled on the grass before him.

Much as he enjoyed these outings, he looked forward to time he could spend by himself. Whenever it was possible, he would escape to the Tatra Mountains for a day or two to hike or ski. He is remembered as a skilled skier and a bit of a daredevil. He did not dress like a daredevil, however. He stood out in baggy pants, old-fashioned lace-up boots, a hooded jacket, and a woolen hat that he would pull down over his ears. Friends brought him skis from the United States made of the latest materials, but he preferred skis made of Polish hickory.

On one such expedition into the Tatras, he met one of the local mountain people. The two men chatted for a time, using the dialect of that remote region, with which Bishop Wojtyla had long been familiar. The bishop offered to share his bread and sausages with the mountain man. The two men sat in a clearing and ate.

"What do you do for a living?" his companion asked him.

"I'm a bishop," said Wojtyla.

The man tossed back his head and laughed. "That's good," he said. "You're a bishop, and I'm the pope."

The same year that Karol was named bishop, Cardinal Angelo Giuseppe Roncalli succeeded Pius XII as pope. He took the name of John XXIII.

Since he was seventy-seven years old at the time, most people believed that Pope John's reign would be short and uneventful. But in 1959 he stunned the Catholic Church by announcing that he intended to call a general council to renew and update Catholic life and doctrine. As he told a visitor, he wanted to open the window and allow fresh air to blow through the Catholic Church.

The pope's announcement was not greeted with enthusiasm. Most cardinals were filled with anxiety. A council was certain to mean change, even upheaval. Vatican administrators did not want change. They hoped the pope would forget the idea.

But Pope John pressed ahead. In October 1962, the bishops of the world assembled at the Vatican for what was officially known as the Second Vatican Council (what is referred to as the First Vatican Council was held in 1870). There were three other sessions, one each autumn until 1965. (Pope John XXIII died in 1963 and was succeeded by Pope Paul VI, who approved the decrees issued after the council ended in 1965.)

The Vatican Council was to have an important influence on Bishop Wojtyla. It was to provide him with additional exposure to individuals whose backgrounds and experiences were vastly different from his own. He has often been described as "a man who visibly grew with the council."

For a time there was some question as to whether Bishop Wojtyla, his fellow bishops, and their superior, Cardinal Wyszynski, would be permitted by the Communist authorities to leave Poland and attend the council sessions. The conflict between state and church had heated up again.

While the oppression did not equal that of the Stalin era, it was a heavy burden nevertheless. Crippling taxes had been imposed on bishops, priests, and nuns. The construction of new churches had been made more difficult. Young men studying for the priesthood were drafted for military service. Articles and books expressing a Catholic point of view were heavily censored. No one would have been surprised if the Polish prelates had been denied the documents necessary for foreign travel.

But the authorities relented. Not only were Cardinal Wyszynski and sixteen of his bishops able to be present at the council sessions, but bishops from several other Iron Curtain countries were also permitted to attend, including four bishops from East Germany, three from Hungary, three from Czechoslovakia, and several from Yugoslavia. Some observers said that this was a tribute to the open-minded attitude of Pope John, who had made it clear that he regarded all men as brothers, a concept that made dialogue with Communism possible.

Shortly before he left for Rome, Bishop Wojtyla addressed parishioners of Cracow who jammed Wawel Cathedral. He revealed his feelings about the council, saying, ". . . what we have learned of the council so far has convinced us that it heralds a real change of direction, a transformation at the heart of the Church."

Bishop Wojtyla was not a typical council member. Most of the council members were specialists in theology; that is, their training had concentrated on the study of the nature of God and religious truths. While he could cope with theological problems, Karol was more of a philosopher. He had studied truth and the principles of all real knowledge. He was calm, and he was rational in debates and discussions.

Moreover, he was a bishop who had remained in close touch with his people. He was well acquainted with modern problems.

It did not take Bishop Wojtyla long to catch the attention of foreign clerics with his command of many languages and his youthful energy. He headed the Eastern Division of the Polish clerical volleyball team and he skied. Some of the bishops were at a disadvantage because council proceedings were conducted in Latin. But this was no handicap for Bishop Wojtyla, who was as skilled in Latin as in French or Italian or Polish.

Little was accomplished at the council's first session in 1962. By the time the bishops had assembled for the second session in the autumn of 1963, Pope John had died. Giovanni Battista Montini, as Pope Paul VI, pledged his active support of the council.

It was during the second council session that Bishop Wojtyla began to make important contributions concerning the Constitution of the Church. When the preliminary discussions began, he urged the assembled bishops to consider the church as the "people of God." What he was saying was that everyone—lay people as well as clerics—was responsible for the mission of the church.

He wanted the church to move away from the idea that authority belonged only to those at the top of the power structure. He introduced the concept of "shared authority."

He also stressed the necessity for proclaiming religious freedom. In this regard he echoed the words of Pope John, who had affirmed that every human being "has the right to worship God in accordance with the dictates of his own conscience and to profess his religion in both private and public."

Living under Communism had given Bishop Wojtyla first-hand experience with atheism, the doctrine holding that there is no God. Indeed, he numbered as friends many people who did not believe in a God. But he preferred to look for a common ground between them. He believed that the church must take men and women as they are. In a speech published in 1976 in *L'Osservatore Roman,* the official Vatican newspaper, Wojtyla said, "One can understand that a man may search and not find; one can understand that he may deny; but it is incomprehensible that a man should be told, 'You may not believe.' "

Early in 1964, Bishop Wojtyla was made Archbishop of Cracow, an advance in status (an archbishop is a bishop of the highest rank) that many people had been expecting. He was, at forty-three, the youngest archbishop in all of Poland. Not since the death of Cardinal Sapieha some thirteen years before had Cracow had an archbishop.

The Archbishop's Palace in Cracow is a magnificent structure. Its spacious, high-ceilinged rooms are decorated with thirteenth-century paintings and other priceless works of art, some dating to Poland's earliest days. Some of the chairs, tables, and other furniture were used by Polish kings. It was the same Palace in which Karol, as a young man studying for the priesthood, had been hidden from the Germans by Archbishop Sapieha.

Karol was expected to move to the Archbishop's Palace after his appointment, but he continued to live in his modest apartment. This upset members of his staff. They felt that the leader of the church in Cracow should live in circumstances that reflected his high office. Time after time they asked Bishop Wojtyla to move, but he shrugged off such suggestions.

When the archbishop left Cracow for a few days, they saw their chance. They went to his apartment, packed up his books, the few articles of clothing he owned, and his personal belongings and brought them to the Archbishop's Palace. When the archbishop returned to Cracow, he was far from pleased with what confronted him. He said nothing at the time, but he later chided those who had been involved.

He was not always punctual. Lunch at the Archbishop's Palace was served at one-thirty. The archbishop would leave his office for the dining room well before one-thirty. But people who wanted to talk with him would post themselves in the corridor through which he had to pass. They knew he never refused anyone who wanted to say a few words. So it would be two o'clock or two-fifteen before the archbishop arrived for lunch.

Wojtyla worked at every opportunity. He had a small table and a reading lamp installed in the rear-seat area of his chauffeur-driven sedan so that he could work as he was being driven from one appointment to the next. Once, on a long trip, trouble developed with the car's electrical system, and the driver asked for permission to switch off Wojtyla's lamp because it was draining power from the battery. "No," said the archbishop. "As long as it shines, we will permit it to shine."

As archbishop, Karol put into action a number of programs that were meant to minister to the social needs of Cracow and its surrounding communities. During the war many hospitals had been destroyed and were never replaced. To enter a hospital for treatment, one had to put one's name on a long waiting list. Archbishop Wojtyla sought to cope with this problem by establishing a bureau to look after the seriously ill. To head it he chose a priest who had been left an invalid by a serious illness. "You're the ideal person," the archbishop told him. "You know what it's like to be ill, and so you will sympathize."

Archbishop Wojtyla also established a Family Institute. He chose a woman who was a psychiatrist and a survivor of the Ravensbruck concentration camp to head it. The Institute was both a clinic that treated medical ills as well as a counseling center. Archbishop Wojtyla visited the Institute daily.

In the evenings, or whenever they had spare time, doctors representing the Institute went to the small villages on the outskirts of Cracow to offer advice on family problems and give talks on the subject of birth control. They favored the rhythm method of birth control, which is based upon the fact that a woman can become pregnant during only a few days in her monthly menstrual cycle. The rhythm method works for some couples, but is generally less effective than artificial birth control methods, which Archbishop Wojtyla and his doctors opposed on moral grounds. Also, birth control pills, at that time, were thought by many to be a health hazard.

Archbishop Wojtyla welcomed the innovations that resulted from the Vatican Council. He was quick to accept the change that mandated that a priest offering mass was now to face the people; previously he had stood with his back to them. And instead of saying the mass in Latin, the priest was now to use the vernacular, or the language native to one's country.

Construction of a new church in the community of Nowa Huta also occupied the archbishop's time. First, some background to this. After World War II had ended and Poland was firmly in Russia's grasp, Stalin ordered that an entire city be built on the outskirts of Cracow to house the workers of the mammoth Lenin steelworks, the largest in all of Europe. The city was to be called Nowa Huta (New Foundry). It was to be the model Communist community.

The tall, concrete apartment buildings started going up, one exactly like the other. A towering statue of Lenin, the Russian revolutionary leader, was installed as the city's centerpiece. Everything was provided—except a church. To the atheistic state, a church was considered unnecessary, a symbol of old superstitious beliefs. Modern socialists had no need for a church. Besides, there were about 200 churches in Cracow, more than enough for a city of its size.

But once the apartment buildings were completed and families started moving in, the people insisted that a church be built. At first, they worshipped in an old building, but they kept demanding more, much to the embarrassment of the local authorities.

Finally, in 1957, permission was granted to build a church in Nowa Huta, and a site was established. The people of the city put up a big cross on the site, a sign that a church was to be built there.

The government changed its mind in 1960, announcing

that the site was to be used instead for the construction of a school. Workers arrived to take down the cross. A riot broke out. The people threw stones at the workers, and the police were called. The police resorted to tear gas and machine guns. Several people were wounded. The rioters were given heavy prison sentences, but the government decided to let the cross stand, at least temporarily.

All of this time Bishop Wojtyla was acting in support of the construction of the church, although he was careful never to say or do anything that might trigger violence. He preached countless sermons on behalf of the church, and he was the moving force behind petitions addressed to local officials that bore the signatures of thousands who hungered to have the church built. And in private conversations with the authorities he pressed for permission to proceed with construction.

A permit was finally granted in 1967 to build a church at another site. But no assistance was given in the form of money or construction materials. The people of Nowa Huta raised the money on their own. People from many parts of the world, not only those in Poland, contributed. Construction began.

In 1977, as a cardinal, Karol Wojtyla dedicated the church before a crowd of 50,000. The struggle to build it had lasted a quarter of a century. The church is constructed of concrete and stone. Circular in form, its imaginative design features a roof topped by a mighty concrete ark. The structure stands in sharp contrast to the somber sameness of Nowa Huta's apartment blocks.

In presiding over the dedication of the new church, Cardinal Wojtyla told a weeping, rejoicing crowd, "This was built as a city without God. But the will of God and the people who work here has prevailed. Let this be a lesson."

CHAPTER

6

IF YOU WERE TO DRAW A CHART SHOWING THE GOVernment of the Catholic Church, it would look like a pyramid. The pope would be at the very top, heading an organization made up of approximately 125 cardinals, 3,700 bishops, 421,000 priests, 986,000 nuns, and approximately 740 million other baptized Catholics.

The pope has absolute authority over church affairs. He can make new church laws or can decide that certain laws be done away with. He appoints cardinals and bishops. He establishes church dioceses, or districts, and approves new religious orders. (An order is a society of priests or nuns, or both, that live under the same set of rules and regulations.) The pope can call an ecumenical council, or a general council, whenever he wishes.

The pope's spiritual powers enable him to absolve persons from certain sins. He can also punish those who disobey his orders or the laws of the church, handing down the sentence of excommunication, wherein a person is cut off from church membership. The pope can also declare a person a saint.

The Curia Romana, or Curia for short, assists the pope in governing the church. The Curia is composed of about 300 men, a good many of them cardinals.

Five hundred years ago, reports of great territorial discoveries were brough to the Vatican and resulted in massive missionary efforts in North and South America, Asia, and Africa. To administer all of the new church activity, various branches of government had to be established. So in 1588 the Curia came into being.

There are nine major departments, called Sacred Congregations, within the Curia. Each is headed by a cardinal. These congregations are responsible for such matters as Catholic education, Catholic doctrine, and missionary efforts.

The base of the church's organizational pyramid is formed by the large number of priests. Women are excluded from the priesthood in the Catholic Church. As recently as 1983, the church declared that "only baptized men can become priests."

Just above the priests are the bishops. The pope appoints bishops, and they are responsible to him. Catholics believe that bishops are the successors to the apostles, the early disciples sent forth by Christ to preach the gospel.

The cardinals are above the bishops and just below the pope in the pyramid. They are appointed by the pope to be his chief advisors. They are usually chosen from the body of bishops.

Although the title of cardinal dates back over a thousand years, it was not until 1150 that the Sacred College of Cardinals was formed. Since 1179, the Sacred College has had the exclusive right of electing the pope. Every Christian nation is represented by at least one member of the college.

A man may be singled out and named a cardinal by

virtue of long and dedicated service in the Curia. Or a likely candidate may be the bishop of a diocese that, by reason of its size and importance, is entitled to be headed by a cardinal.

There is an element of chance in the process. One has to be in the right place at the right time. It is also important to have friends in Rome in high places. But, for the most part, those who are ultimately chosen are men of superior ability who are hard-working, good executives and are politically informed.

During 1967 Pope Paul VI decided to increase the number of cardinals from 83 to 120. On May 29 that year, the names of 27 new cardinals were announced. Archbishop Karol Wojtyla of Cracow was one of them.

Cardinal Wojtyla journeyed to Rome for the installation ceremonies. On his return to Cracow, he offered mass at Wawel Cathedral. A reception was held in his honor after the mass. "It's the last time I shall be a nuisance to you," he said to a friend jokingly. "After all, I can't go any higher." Events, of course, were to prove him wrong.

Although he was now a cardinal, Wojtyla made no change in the way he dressed, continuing to wear a plain black cassock without any of a cardinal's red trim. His room was simply furnished. He was still available to anyone who wanted to see him. He did, however, give up his bicycle and agree to be driven when necessary.

As a cardinal, Wojtyla was frequently overshadowed by seventy-seven year-old Stefan Wyszynski, the Cardinal Primate of Poland, or the highest ranking Polish church leader. The Polish Catholic Church had grown spectacularly under Wyszynski's reign. By the late 1970s, it was twice as large as when the Communists had taken over the government in the late 1940s. Attendance at Sunday mass in many parishes was so heavy that pastors had to schedule nonstop services throughout the day and into the evening.

The Communist regime and the church had come to look upon their relationship in very realistic terms. The

Communist officials realized that from 85 to 90 percent of the Polish population was Catholic, and that the great majority of these people were devoted churchgoers. These factors made the church a powerful ideological force. But church officials fully realized that their power was limited and that they could push the government only so far. Soviet tanks had been called in to crush uprisings in Czechoslovakia, Hungary, and in Poznan in Poland. They could be called in again.

While Cardinals Wyszynski and Wojtyla were in perfect agreement on basic positions, they contrasted sharply on the way in which they went about achieving their goals. The tough-minded Wyszynski was unbending in his dealings with the Communist authorities. He never hesitated in denouncing them or their pronouncements.

Cardinal Wojtyla was cooler. He recognized the Communist regime in Poland as a fact of life. He was more tactful and more understanding in dealing with the government, although on fundamental issues he remained as firm as a rock.

In time the Communist authorities came to see Wojtyla as the greater threat—and with good reason. Through his spiritual depth and intelligence, his ability as a speaker and his shrewdness, Cardinal Wojtyla came to be the very symbol of Poland's struggle against Communism.

Cardinal Wojtyla never sought preeminence. He once asked a group of Italian journalists how many Italian cardinals skied. "None," he was told.

"In Poland," he said, "40 percent of the cardinals ski."

Someone reminded him that there were only two Polish cardinals. "Precisely," said Wojtyla, "Wyszynski counts for 60 percent."

Over the next several years, Cardinal Wojtyla traveled widely. He visited Australia, where he was photographed feeding kangaroos. In New Guinea he was pictured with a group of feathered tribesmen. He visited France, Belgium, and West Germany several times. And, of course, there were many trips to Rome, to the Vatican.

Cardinal Wojtyla made two trips to the United States, one in 1969 and the other in 1976. His visit in 1976 lasted five weeks, during which time he and seventeen Polish bishops crisscrossed North America, lecturing at universities, attending receptions in their honor, offering masses, and addressing Polish communities. New York, Philadelphia, Baltimore, Cincinnati, Detroit, Chicago, Los Angeles, and Buffalo, and Toronto and Hamilton in Ontario, Canada, were some of the cities they visited.

Cardinal Wojtyla and the bishops crossed the Atlantic in three separate airplanes on orders from Cardinal Wyszynski, who did not want most of the leaders of the Polish Catholic Church traveling on one plane. The group spent their first day in the United States in Washington, where they visited the Catholic University.

The next day they journeyed north by train to Philadelphia. A group of Polish-American priests waited to greet them at Philadelphia's Thirtieth Street Station. When Cardinal Wojtyla stepped from the train, mouths hung open and eyebrows shot up. He was wearing, as was his custom, a long, flowing cassock. Most of the bishops with him also wore cassocks. The cassock, although once worn by American Catholic priests, is rarely seen today.

"He looked so out of place," one priest recalled. "Heads were turning to look at him. People stared. He caused a traffic jam outside the railroad station."

Cardinal Wojtyla later explained to his hosts why he and many of his bishops wore cassocks. "In Poland, it is worn everywhere," he said, "not because of its convenience, but because of what the cassock means. In a Communist country, the cassock is a sign. It makes the priest visible; it is a reminder."

In Philadelphia Cardinal Wojtyla renewed his friendship with Cardinal John Joseph Krol, the city's archbishop. The two men had much in common. Not only were both Polish, but the forebears of each were from the Tatra Mountain

65

In 1976, as a cardinal, Karol Wojtyla led a group of Polish bishops on an extended tour of the United States. Here he is pictured with Bishop Edward Head of Buffalo. (United Press International)

region of southern Poland. (Cardinal Krol, however, had been born in Cleveland.) They were both appointed cardinals on the same day. They both shared the same views of the church in the modern world.

Cardinal Wojtyla and his colleagues attracted their biggest audiences in Chicago. Chicago has a larger Polish population than any other city outside Poland.

In Los Angeles Cardinal Wojtyla visited Our Lady of the Bright Mount, the only Polish parish in that city. He met with 300 Polish Americans in the parish hall and listened to their stories of life in California. He also met with representatives of the Catholic press in Los Angeles. He spoke out in strong terms on the subject of abortion, which had become a highly controversial issue in the United States.

Abortion, the ending of a pregnancy before birth, results in the death of the embryo, or fetus. One aspect of the controversy concerns whether a woman should be permitted by law to have an abortion and, if so, under what circumstances. Another aspect centers on whether, and to what extent, laws should protect the unborn child's right to life. Arguments against abortion center upon the belief that an abortion is the unjustified killing of an unborn child.

The Catholic Church opposes abortion, as do some Protestant and Jewish groups. Adherents of Buddhism and Hinduism also oppose abortion.

The abortion controversy had gained intensity three years earlier, in 1973, when the United States Supreme Court ruled that states could not forbid a woman to have an abortion during the first three months of pregnancy if her doctor approved the operation. During her second three months of pregnancy, states could regulate abortions only to protect a woman's health.

The Supreme Court's ruling took most Americans by surprise. Many hailed the decision. They said it would put an end to the tragedies of unwanted motherhood.

Some condemned the Supreme Court's ruling. "It is all reminiscent of the 'what-is-useful-is-good' philosophy of

German medicine in the 1930s," said Nick Thimmesch in *Newsweek* magazine, a philosophy that "helped bring on the slaughter of millions of human beings a few years later."

Cardinal Wojtyla, in speaking to representatives of the Catholic press in Los Angeles, declared that the consequences of abortion "are dangerous, not only for Christian morality and family, but also for the nation. Abortion violates the Fifth Commandment—Thou shalt not kill."

Many people declared that the right to an abortion gives a woman the freedom to make a choice. To these people, Cardinal Wojtyla said that freedom is not doing what one wants. "It is," he stated, "to realize and know true good—and then choose true good."

During his visit to the United States Cardinal Wojtyla also managed to fit Great Falls, Montana, into his schedule. He went to Great Falls even though there are few Catholics and even fewer Poles there. His reason was to see a close friend, Monsignor Joseph Gluszek.

Monsignor Gluszek, who was twelve years older than Cardinal Wojtyla, had been brought up and had gone to school in Wadowice, where the cardinal was born, and they had many friends in common. He later became a priest in the Cracow diocese. On the first day of World War II in 1939, Father Gluszek was arrested and taken to a concentration camp, where he was to spend the next six years. After the war, he remained in Germany, working with Polish refugees there.

In 1950 Father Gluszek was sent to the United States as a visiting priest and then decided to remain here. He became an American citizen in 1956 and was eventually assigned to the Great Falls parish in Montana.

Although Father Gluszek and Cardinal Wojtyla did not meet until 1969, they had corresponded with one another through the years. The cardinal's letters talked about the churches in Cracow and the priests and their duties. He never failed to inquire about Father Gluszek's health. "His kindness is always there. It's hard to find a man of such a big heart," Father Gluszek said.

Officially, Monsignor Gluszek was still a priest attached to the Cracow diocese and only on loan to Great Falls, Montana, a fact that Cardinal Wojtyla noted when addressing Monsignor Gluszek's congregation. "Those people in Philadelphia told me, 'Don't go to Montana because there is nothing to see.' I told them I don't care if there is anything to see or not—I have my priest there and I want to see *him!*"

"Boy! That was one of my proudest moments," Monsignor Gluszek was to say afterward.

As a cardinal, Wojtyla also became a familiar figure in Rome. The contributions he made to the many bishops' synods, or formal meetings, held there in the decade following the Vatican Council stamped him as one who understood the problems of the church, not only in his own country, but in every part of the world. At a meeting of the bishops in 1974, he outlined these problems in concise terms. In Africa there was a need to express the gospel in rites and languages that could be understood by the local citizens. In Asia the concern was with non-Christian religions, chiefly Buddhism and Hinduism. Latin America was intent on using Christian doctrine to attain social and political gains for oppressed people. Europe and North America were worried about an ever-increasing emphasis on worldly things; all that was religious and spiritual was diminishing in importance. Elsewhere in the world Cardinal Wojtyla noted a "systematic . . . atheism that denied any place for God in the life of an individual or society."

In 1976 Cardinal Wojtyla was invited to preach the Lenten retreat for Pope Paul VI, the cardinals and bishops of the Curia, and the members of the Vatican household. (A retreat is a period of seclusion devoted to prayer and meditation.) In his talks, Cardinal Wojtyla demonstrated his wide range of knowledge, not only concerning philosophy and theology but in literature as well. His sermons revealed that

69

the Nazi occupation of Poland and living under atheistic Communism had left indelible imprints upon his character, as had the Vatican Council and its recommendations.

The sermons he had delivered at the pope's Lenten retreat in 1976, his talks before the bishops' synods, and his experience at the Second Vatican Council enabled Wojtyla to become known and respected by many church leaders. So had the fact that he had traveled extensively and had acted as a host in Cracow for visiting cardinals.

During his years as priest, bishop, archbishop, and cardinal, he had expressed his thoughts and views in well over 100 articles, essays, poems, and plays. There could be no doubt about where he stood on all of the issues that mattered.

On August 6, 1978, Cardinal Wojtyla was brought the news that Pope Paul VI had died. He went to the monastery at Kalwaria to offer mass for him. Immediately after, he left for Rome and the conclave of cardinals that elected Cardinal Albino Luciani as Pope John Paul I.

When Cardinal Wojtyla returned to Cracow, he appeared relaxed and cheerful. He went to Kalwaria to say a Mass of Thanksgiving.

At the time, the church in Poland was involved in a struggle with the government over access to mass media. To the press, radio, and television of Poland, long controlled by the government, it was as if the Catholic Church did not exist.

A pastoral letter from the Polish bishops was read at all Polish churches on Sunday, September 17; it called for a lifting of the government's ban. The letter, certainly influenced by Cardinal Wojtyla, stated: "The mass communications media are abused in order to impose one kind of view only and one behavior pattern only, and to exert power over people. To ignore our opinion is to treat us as objects to be manipulated at will by those who have acquired power over the citizens."

The bishops asked that, at the very least, the govern-

Cardinal Wojtyla at St. Peter's Square in Rome in 1978.
(United Press International)

John Paul II not long after his installation as pope in 1978. (Polish Daily News)

ment permit a weekly Sunday mass to be broadcast "for those who are ill or suffering."

Cardinal Wojtyla signed the letter. It was the last document he would sign as Cardinal of Cracow. Within two weeks, Pope John Paul I had died. Ironically, the ban of the broadcasting of religious services was first lifted to broadcast the installation ceremonies of Karol Wojtyla as pope.

CHAPTER

7

AT FIFTY-EIGHT, HE WAS CONSIDERED "TOO YOUNG" to be elected pope. In addition, he was not Italian, and no "foreigner" had managed to lay claim to the chair of St. Peter for more than five centuries. It was an astonishing election, one that the new pope himself described as "an act of courage" on the part of the assembled cardinals.

When the news that Karol Wojtyla had been elected pope was received in Wadowice, his hometown, the people were stunned. Many rushed to friends' apartments or even out onto the streets, kissing one another and weeping tears of joy.

The friend with whom young Karol had practiced soccer was in the kitchen of his apartment. His wife was watching television in another room. He heard the words, "We have a pope." What followed was blotted out by his wife's shrieks. He rushed into the room to see what had happened. His wife was close to collapse. "My God! My

God!'' she cried out. ''Do you know what they've done? They've made Lolek pope!''

While Polish Catholics were pleased and proud that one of their own had become the world's best known religious leader, Communist authorities in Poland received the news with some alarm. They feared that the naming of a Polish pope might arouse the hopes of the people for more freedom. Communist leaders also realized that Karol Wojtyla's election was going to mean that their nation would be getting increased attention from the media. Communist governments generally do not like reporters and camera crews poking around their countries.

In the days that followed the election of John Paul II, the press made many attempts to define and explain him. It was brought to light that he had once worked in a stone quarry, that he had been a member of Poland's anti-Nazi underground, the pastor of a country church, and a professor of ethics. He was cited as a skier, a hiker, and a mountain climber.

But most of all, he was a Pole. He had endured the decades of oppression and confrontation that being Polish implied. That fact, more than any other, would color his papacy.

At his inauguration mass, he seemed to be speaking directly to the leaders of Eastern European nations and the Soviet Union when he said, ''Open wide the doors to Christ. To His saving power, open the boundaries of states, economic and political systems, the vast fields of culture, civilization, and development. Do not be afraid.''

John Paul was putting a simple question to Communist leaders: What are you afraid of? Why do you not trust the people in whose name you claim to act?

Some popes have tried to control the Curia tightly, even going so far as to involve themselves in the smallest details of government. Others have been content to make only important decisions.

John Paul took an interest only in those matters that concerned subjects in which he was deeply involved. He was never reluctant to make decisions when they were needed. But for day-to-day contact with the Curia, John Paul relied on Cardinal Agostino Casaroli.

After the death in 1979 of Cardinal Jean Paul Villot, the Vatican Secretary of State, John Paul named Casaroli to the papacy's second highest post. Casaroli had worked with the Curia all of his life. He had been a special envoy for Pope Paul VI, assigned to negotiate with Iron Curtain countries. The then Archbishop Wojtyla first came to the Vatican's attention after a long period that Casaroli spent in Poland in 1967. Following Casaroli's return to Rome, Wojtyla was named a cardinal. Today, few men are as close to the pope as Cardinal Casaroli.

John Paul appointed Father Stanislaw Dziwisz as his private secretary. Although barely thirty-four, Father Dziwisz had been with John Paul for thirteen years. Father Dziwisz spoke the pope's language. It was said he thought the pope's thoughts. The two men were as close as father and son.

Father John Magee, also close to the pope, was another private secretary. From Ireland, Father Magee once served in Nigeria as a missionary. He was courteous, quick to smile, and one of the most popular of the pope's staff members.

Fathers Dziwisz and Magee shepherd the pope through his daily schedule. The pope awakens at five o'clock, dresses himself in a white linen cassock and dons a white skullcap, then prays privately in his bedroom before offering mass in his private chapel at seven. He often invites small groups of visiting priests or bishops to attend the mass. The pope then sits down to a breakfast of coffee, buns, and perhaps sausage or fried ham. There are usually breakfast guests. But the pope is not simply entertaining; he is looking for information. He questions his guests and listens to what they have to say.

When breakfast is over, the pope takes his private elevator to his third floor study. He spends the next two hours reading and writing. Whereas he once was able to use this time to read poetry, or even write it, he now works on papal messages. He often writes them out in longhand in Polish. They are then sent out to secretaries for translation into the appropriate language.

At eleven o'clock the pope prepares to assume his role as Vatican head of state, receiving diplomatic representatives from various parts of the world. He also sees church groups during this time. These semiprivate audiences are held in the resplendent Clementine Room in the Vatican Palace. A monsignor addresses the waiting guests: "When the Holy Father comes in, he will want to know that we are very happy to see him. And so it would not be inappropriate for us to begin to applaud as soon as he enters. I'd like to suggest that when you approach the Holy Father, instead of instinctively kissing his ring as you would normally do, shake his hand and engage his eyes."

Through the reign of Pope Pius XII, who died in 1958, it was usual for priests, bishops, and cardinals, when meeting the pope, to kiss his ring and the toe of his slipper, thus signifying their loyalty to him. Pope John XXIII did away with the kissing ritual but allowed his ring to be kissed in private audiences. At public audiences he pulled his hand back whenever possible. Paul VI adopted this attitude. He was even known to slap softly at people's hands to prevent his own hand from being grabbed. John Paul allows the ring to be kissed in official ceremonies, such as when cardinals are pledging their allegiance to him, but in semiprivate and public audiences he will pull his hand away.

In the early weeks of his papacy, there were several skirmishes between Pope John Paul and Vatican officials, most of whom are deeply bound in custom and tradition. One involved the protocol prelate, usually a priest or monsignor, who stands at the pope's side during audiences. It was usual for this assistant to lay a hand on the pope's arm and say, "basta," Italian for enough, when he felt the pope had taken long enough with the person or group to whom he was speaking. But John Paul paid no attention to the signal and kept talking for as long as he wished. The word "basta" is no longer heard during papal audiences.

John Paul has not always been the victor in these battles of wits. There was the clothing issue, for instance. Vatican officials fretted over the clothing that John Paul brought with him to the Vatican. Much of the material was frayed or had been darned and patched. Worse, when he lifted his arms at an early audience, one could see his undershirt. Vatican officials were deeply distressed. Papal tailors were set to work making him white cassocks and a dozen long-sleeved shirts with French cuffs, which he was asked to wear. Now no one is upset when he raises his arms. The pope's tailors also provided him with a wool cardigan that he wears over his cassock and beneath his cape for outdoor appearances in cold weather.

The pope continues with the semiprivate audiences until one-thirty or so. Then he has lunch, usually a bowl of soup and a sandwich. He almost always has luncheon guests, often a bishop or other high-ranking religious figure. Sometimes lay people are also invited. They are invariably male; female guests are rare.

The pope puts aside all official duties after lunch for some relaxation—a rest or a walk, or perhaps both. When he walks, he covers at least a mile and sometimes as much as two miles at a very brisk pace through the Vatican gardens. One of his secretaries usually accompanies him. They are closely trailed by security guards.

Exercise is very important to the pope. Not long after his installation, he requested that a swimming pool be built for him at the papal summer residence at Castel Gondolfo. Papal critics charged that the pool was an extravagance. The pope, indicating how seriously he looked upon the benefits to be derived from swimming, replied, "Another conclave would be more expensive."

In the afternoon John Paul either works with his advisors or schedules public appearances in or near Rome. He takes his role as the Bishop of Rome very seriously. He regularly visits local schools, churches, and hospitals. He invites local priests to the Vatican Palace to discuss their problems with him. Some Vatican officials say that the pope is seen too often in public, that he is becoming too familiar to the people of Rome. But his supporters argue that contact is important, that it earns him the approval of Catholics and non-Catholics alike.

On Wednesday afternoons the pope conducts a public audience, addressing a group of several thousand people. Afterward, he speaks to small clusters of them in several languages, singing their religious songs and lingering to touch and bless as many of them as time allows. He never appears rushed during these audiences; he moves easily but deliberately among the pilgrims, offering his hand, nodding, and smiling.

Out of the public eye the pope becomes quite a different person. He is brisk and efficient in dealing with his Vatican staff, sometimes scheduling as many as four fifteen-minute meetings in an hour. Archbishops and cardinals who are ushered into the pope's study find John Paul with several folders of the appropriate information in front of him. He wastes little time in small talk, getting down to business immediately.

During the day the pope may also hold private audiences with foreign dignitaries. These have included audiences with King Baudouin of Belgium, King Hussein of Jordan, and Soviet Foreign Minister Andrei Gromyko. When President Carter was President of the United States, the pope welcomed Rosalynn and Amy Carter, the wife and daughter of the President.

Sometimes the pope has dinner with his secretaries. But he will also dine alone, scanning newspaper headlines while keeping an eye on television newscasts. Following this, he works on church matters until he retires.

At eleven o'clock the huge iron gates of the Vatican

Pope John Paul receives a basketball as a gift from a schoolboy during a visit to a Rome suburb in 1978. (United Press International)

swing shut. Some popes have been virtual prisoners of the Vatican, cut off from personal contact and constrained by centuries of tradition and custom. Not Pope John Paul. Being pope has given him greater freedom to act and to speak. One of his close friends who attended his installation ceremony in Rome observed on his return to Cracow: "Now, at last, he is where he ought to be. He is more truly himself than he has ever been."

Popes speak and write continually. When a pope, acting as the head of the church, speaks or writes concerning matters of faith or morals, Catholics believe that he cannot possibly commit an error. He is said to have divine assistance when he speaks in this manner.

One month after his election as pope, John Paul wrote his first encyclical. An encyclical is an official letter written by the pope to all the bishops of the church. It is the method by which popes clarify the mission of the church and explain its teachings.

Pope John Paul's first encyclical emphasized the dignity of man. It sharply criticized capitalistic "consumer societies," which transform man into "the slave of things, the slave of economic systems . . . the slave of his own products."

The pope's strongest words, however, were directed against totalitarian governments that use torture, terrorism, and discrimination to deny basic human rights to citizens. Although he did not mention any countries by name, the pope made a special plea for those societies that grant "only atheism the right of citizenship."

The pope also spoke about celibacy in his letter. When a young man becomes a Catholic priest, he takes a vow that he will not marry, that he will remain celibate. The church's rule concerning celibacy dates back more than a thousand years. It was an attempt to turn members of the clergy into monk-like figures, to separate them from the vested interests of feudal society. In Eastern Orthodox churches, bishops must be celibate, but priests are permitted to marry before being ordained. Protestant churches reject celibacy.

The matter of celibacy within the church had become highly controversial in the United States in the 1960s. During that period and well into the decade that followed, the church suffered from a continual loss of priests, many of whom wanted to leave the priesthood in order to marry. Pope Paul VI received 32,357 requests in 15 years from priests asking for release from their vows. He granted all but 1,033 of the requests. It was argued at the time that if the Catholic Church were to relax the celibacy rule, the flood of young men leaving the priesthood would be halted.

There is no doubt that the rule of celibacy could be lifted by papal decree. No one expects the pope to permit the marriage of any priest already ordained. The question is, might he permit, in some instances, men who are already married to be ordained? Some former Lutheran ministers, married men, were ordained with papal approval under Pius XIII.

But Pope John Paul, in his encyclical, resisted whatever pressure may have then existed to make the rule of celibacy less strict. "To be able to serve others worthily and effectively, we must be able to master ourselves," he wrote. And he urged every priest to be "faithful to the bond that he has accepted."

A month later the pope spoke out again on the subject of celibacy in the thirty-five page letter to the Catholic clergy. By voluntarily rejecting natural fatherhood, the pope's letter said, the priest is seeking "another fatherhood" as a spiritual shepherd for others. "The priesthood cannot be renounced because of the difficulties that we meet and the sacrifices asked of us."

The pope's stand on celibacy was an indication of what was to come. He was planning to set forth and teach basic Catholic truths. They would not be a matter for debate.

CHAPTER 8

ALMOST IMMEDIATELY AFTER TAKING OFFICE, JOHN Paul II declared that he was eager to travel. "I would like to take God's message everywhere," he said. He mentioned that he wanted to visit his native Poland, of course, and also the Soviet Union, Egypt, Lebanon, Ireland, the United States, and Latin America.

Many of the countries on the pope's list were torn by strife. John Paul hoped that he would be able to fulfill a role as peacemaker by visiting them. But he would also travel as the head of the Catholic Church; in so doing he would provide the church with new direction where it was needed and would strengthen the ardor of its worshippers.

Through the centuries most popes have seen a necessity for travel, although there have been some exceptions. Saint Peter journeyed from Jerusalem to become the first Bishop of Rome. Medieval popes traveled to northern Italy, Gaul (in what is now Western Europe), and Germany to spread the word of God.

As the power of the papacy grew during the Middle Ages, the church acquired control of several provinces in central Italy that came to be known as Papal States. These remained under church control until 1870, when they were confiscated by the state. To show their resistance, Pope Pius IX and the three popes who followed him over the next sixty years made themselves virtual prisoners of the Vatican. Pope Pius XII, whose reign began in 1939, managed to leave the Vatican on occasion, but only to motor the fifteen or so miles to Castel Gondolfo to escape Rome's summer heat.

John XXIII resumed the tradition of papal travel. He visited the Byzantine monastery at Grottaferrata just south of Rome, and nearby churches and shrines. He traveled by rail to "Holy House" at Loretto in northern Italy.

Paul VI, who succeeded John XXIII in 1963, was a world traveler. His first pilgrimage was to Jerusalem. He became the first pope to visit Latin America and the United States and to speak before the United Nations. He took pride in referring to himself as the "pilgrim pope."

When Karol Wojtyla was raised to the papacy in 1978, he spoke of his great love and respect for John XXIII and Paul VI. He was particularly impressed by Paul's concept of himself as a pilgrim, and he made up his mind to assume that role.

His first two foreign trips were planned for the early months of 1979. His first would take him to Mexico; then he would visit Poland.

The Catholic Church in Mexico and, indeed, throughout Latin America, was troubled and confused. Some 300 million of the world's 740 million baptized Catholics live in Latin America. Most of them are desperately poor, but they lack the political power needed to change their status.

The Catholic Church had been identified with the ruling elite in Latin America for centuries. The year 1968 marked a turning point. Calls for political and economic jus-

*Pope John Paul (lower left) blesses a crowd of worshippers
numbering in the hundreds of thousands during his visit
to Mexico in 1979.
(United Press International)*

tice were issued at the Conference of Latin American Bishops (CELAM) held at Medellin, Colombia, that year.

Pope Paul VI visited the conference to restate the church's position concerning economic justice. He urged political caution and denounced violent tactics. But the assembled bishops went further. They issued statements linking capitalism with "institutionalized violence" and the "imperialism of money." They called on the church to maintain "solidarity with the poor."

In the years that followed the Medellin conference, angry debate raged over the political role of priests. Some younger priests openly adopted Communist ideals under the banner of a "liberation theology." Latin American conservatives retaliated. An estimated 850 priests, nuns, and lay people were abducted, killed, or exiled in Latin America in the decade after Medellin.

The Latin American bishops scheduled another conference, their third, at Puebla, Mexico, in January 1979. Pope John Paul was making the trip to Mexico to open the conference.

The appearance loomed as a political mine field for the pope. How could he not support the efforts of the Catholic Church to liberate people from hunger and poverty? But to do so in Latin America might be taken as an endorsement of Communist solutions.

The pope's decision to go to Mexico was a bold one, inasmuch as church-state relations there had been riddled with conflict for more than three centuries. The Catholic religion was planted in Mexico in 1524 by Franciscan friars who befriended the Indians, then newly conquered by the Spanish. But the priesthood soon allied itself with the Spanish overlords. It later became an arm of the Spanish Crown and an opponent of independence. When Spanish rule was overthrown in 1821, and Mexico became an independent state, the church was punished. Under the constitutions of 1857 and 1917, all church property was seized, no new religious orders were permitted, and each of the Mexican states was given the power to determine how many priests could serve in its territory.

The antagonism between church and state has lasted to this day. Mexico was the only country in Latin America that did not maintain diplomatic relations with the Vatican. And foreign clergymen were not permitted to celebrate mass in Mexico, nor were priests allowed to wear their robes in public. The Mexican government had granted the pope a special privilege by allowing him to do both during his visit.

The pope traveled to Mexico in a chartered DC-10. He was given a window seat covered in white velvet in the aircraft's forward compartment. His secretary, Father Dziwisz, sat next to him. Four seats were left empty, to be used for conferences with aides. Seats in the middle cabin of the plane were reserved for the pope's staff members. Newspaper and television reporters were in the third section.

Not long after the aircraft had reached cruising altitude, the pope went back to visit the journalists. He chatted with them and answered their questions in five different languages.

"Do you enjoy the papacy?" he was asked.

"I enjoy working. It is my unique life to concentrate all the strength I have on this job."

"Do you plan to visit the United States?" another newsman wanted to know.

"I suppose it will be necessary. But the time has not been fixed."

The pope made a brief stopover in the Dominican Republic, the West Indies nation that is part of the island of Hispaniola. It was there that the first Catholic missionaries to the Americas said mass in 1494 during Columbus's second voyage. It was also in what is now the Dominican Republic that the first cathedral and convent in the Western Hemisphere were built.

At the airport the pope knelt to kiss the ground. He later celebrated mass in the main square of Santo Domingo, the capital, for a crowd estimated at 300,000.

89

When the pope's plane landed in Mexico, the first people to greet him were Mexican President José Lopez Portillo and his wife. Under the nation's diplomatic regulations, which reflected still existing ill-feeling between church and state, the pope was an "unofficial" guest of the country. The president shook the pope's hand; there was no warm embrace, an unusual omission for an important visitor to a Latin country. But the Mexican people never held back. Millions greeted the pope's masses, motorcades, and festivals with an overwhelming display of warmth. A Mexico City journalist would say, "It was the greatest success any foreign leader has ever scored in Mexico."

In the Zocalo, Mexico City's huge central square, there were loud cheers for "Juan Pablo" and banners reading CHRISTIANITY SI, SOCIALISM NO. Traffic and business came to a standstill. The pope entered the Metropolitan Cathedral to offer—in near-perfect Spanish—the first papal mass in Mexican history. (He had spent an hour a day for several weeks brushing up on his Spanish.)

The following day, when the pope rode across the city to the shrine of the Virgin of Guadalupe, a shrine that has been called the spiritual center of Mexico, the turnout of people defied counting. Police estimated that five million Mexicans stood in the broiling sun along his route. Near hysteria erupted in spots as people jostled to catch a glimpse of him.

In a sermon delivered at the Guadalupe Shrine, John Paul directed his remarks to nuns and priests in the audience. "You must stop seeking new horizons and experiences," he told the nuns. He criticized them for thinking that action could be a substitute for prayer.

He warned the nuns to be careful in their choice of companions. It was a reminder that they should not seek out those who support a theology of liberation. Finally, he told the nuns that they should pray more.

The nuns were filled with dismay. Some seemed on the brink of tears.

Wearing a straw sombrero, Pope John Paul II smiles as he hugs a young child during his six-day visit to Mexico. (United Press International)

Then John Paul turned toward the priests. "You are priests and members of religious orders, not social or political leaders," he declared. The priests sat as if stunned.

In the days that followed, the pope was greeted with showers of confetti, fireworks, floating balloons, and flocks of white doves. Street peddlers hawked photos, pins, and T-shirts bearing the pope's portrait.

When the pope traveled to Puebla from Mexico City to address the continent-wide meeting of bishops, much of the eighty-one mile route was lined with people. Near the Cathedral of Guadalajara, a crippled teen-aged girl waited, hoping to meet the pope. The pope missed her in the press of the crowd. Someone whispered to him about the girl. He plunged into the crowd in search of her but never found her.

When the pope addressed the bishops and other members of the clergy, he made it clear that he rejected the idea of priestly activism based on a Communist philosophy. The idea of Christ as "a political figure, as a revolutionary, as a subversive man from Nazareth" did not tally with the church's teachings, he stated.

The pope insisted that the church speak out when "the growing wealth of a few parallels the growing poverty of the many." But he sharply criticized priests who identified the Kingdom of God with the struggles of the oppressed to the extent that they created a people's Catholicism "to rival the institutional Church."

The pope also emphasized that political tasks were better left to lay people. In another address he told a large gathering of the clergy, "Be priests, not social workers or political leaders. . . ."

The pope pushed himself tirelessly during his trip. He seemed really to love the crowds, the 'oceans of people,' as they were described. The millions who pressed to see him showed a depth of religious feeling that had managed to survive more than a century of church-state hostilities.

But to many of those in the forefront of the struggle for

human rights and economic justice in Latin America, the pope's spectacular visit was something of a disappointment. He seemed not to understand some of the special problems of Latin America. He made no reference to the church leaders who worked hand-in-glove with dictators or military regimes. He said nothing about the priests who had been murdered by terrorists who sometimes represented these same governments. One bishop noted that the pope's words would certainly be used as an excuse to suppress social action on the part of priests and nuns.

Progressive leaders in Latin America would continue to press for human rights and social justice, for the ideals underscored at the Medellin in 1968. But were they supported by the pope? They could not be sure.

CHAPTER

9

KAROL WOJTYLA RETURNED TO POLAND IN JUNE 1979. His nine-day visit marked the first time a Catholic pope had ever visited a Communist country. It also made for one of the most stirring human dramas of recent times as defiant Christians directly confronted the power of Communism.

The pope flew from Rome to Warsaw in a chartered Boeing-727 jet. His anxiety was such that he could eat very little breakfast. As soon as the plane landed at a military airfield outside Warsaw, seventy-seven-year-old Cardinal Wyszynski mounted the steps and entered the cabin. Not long after, John Paul stepped from the plane, dropped to his knees, and kissed his native soil.

The pope rode into Warsaw in an open van. For days people had been flocking into the city on roads and railway lines in the hope of catching a glimpse of him. The London *Daily Mail* called it ''a human tidal wave . . . probably the greatest movement of population in the contemporary history of Europe." Hundreds of thousands cheered the pope's motorcade. Countless church bells rang out a joyous welcome.

The high point of the day was an open-air mass in Warsaw's Victory Square. Half a million people were there, clapping ceaselessly. The pope raised his arms in greeting, waited a moment, and the clapping stopped.

Then John Paul began to speak, his rich and powerful voice echoing through the square. "The exclusion of Christ from the history of man is an act against man," he declared. "Without Christ, it is impossible to understand the history of Poland, especially the history of a people who have passed or are passing through this land." And in reference to Poland's long struggle for freedom, he said, "There can be no Europe without the independence of Poland marked upon the map."

Here was a clear and open statement of the fact that Communism could not expect ultimately to triumph. If a Polish priest had made such a declaration, he would have risked imprisonment.

As the pope spoke, he fought back tears. Again and again, his sermon was interrupted by chants of "We want God! We want God!"

The pope spent the first part of his visit at the ancient monastery of Jasna Gora in Czestochowa, where the Black Madonna, Poland's holiest icon, is kept. The icon is a painting of Mary and the infant Jesus. According to legend, the picture was painted by the Apostle Luke on the wooden planks of a table owned by Joseph, husband of Mary. It is called the "Black" Madonna because the faces of Mary and Jesus are dark, typical of paintings of Middle Eastern origin. The icon is regarded as both the symbol and protector of the Polish nation.

During his stay in Czestochowa, the pope addressed the bishops of Poland. He declared that religious liberty is one of the "fundamental human rights" and directed the bishops to be firm in their struggle with the authorities to assure

The "Black Madonna," symbol of Polish Catholicism.
(Polish Daily News)

normal conditions for the church. "Normal conditions" would mean legal recognition for the church, access to the press and television, an end to censorship of church publications, job equality for Catholics, and the freedom to build more churches.

The pope endorsed these goals and added protests of his own. He fumed about the border guards who turned back thousands of Catholics who wanted to see him. And he expressed disappointment that the government had blacked out news of his visit on television and in the press throughout Eastern Europe. In an age of "declared freedom and exchange of information," the pope said, it is "difficult to think that any Pole, any Slav, cannot hear me."

Throughout the visit the pope plunged among the people whenever he could. He kissed babies and raised young children high in the air. He shook hands and hugged and blessed the old. He sang from the altar and joked from the pulpit. He wept often, sometimes out of joy, other times in sorrow, at the suffering of his people.

One night in the city of Gniezno, after an outdoor mass for 100,000 young people, he began to lead them in a medley of popular tunes. The youngsters pleaded with him for one encore after another. They would not let him leave. Finally, he picked up the microphone and half sang to them, "Your buses are ready. Your buses are ready."

In Wadowice he returned to see the two-room apartment where he had been born. He greeted Helena Szczepanska, an eighty-year-old former neighbor, who had been young Lolek's baby-sitter. She recalled rocking his carriage in the small courtyard below the family apartment and said that her only complaint with him was that he ran around too much.

For many outside Poland, the most moving moments of the pope's trip came when he visited Auschwitz, the one-time Nazi concentration camp. His pilgrimage there, the first by a pope, was a sorrowful journey watched by half a million people who sang sad hymns.

John Paul said mass in the railyards at Birkenau, near Auschwitz, where four million people were herded from cattle cars to the gas chambers. Priests who had been prisoners at the camps celebrated the mass with him.

He knelt in silence before the infamous death wall at Auschwitz, where thousands of inmates had been lined up and shot. He called attention to a Hebrew commemoration plaque and said, "That very people that received from God the commandment, 'Thou shalt not kill,' experienced in a special measure what is meant by killing."

The pope was tired and hoarse as his trip drew to an end. He had delivered about forty speeches, celebrated masses at almost every stop, kissed and hugged hundreds of children, and had been seen and heard by as many as fifteen million people, or almost one Pole out of every two.

In his final address to the industrial workers of Nowa Huta, the pope recalled the long struggle to build a church amidst the apartment towers and tall smokestacks of the model Communist town. "Though I am in Rome," he promised the audience, "I am still among you."

As soon as the pope left, government authorities launched a crackdown. Factory managers and school teachers who failed to keep their workers or students from joining the throngs that had greeted the pope were fired from their jobs. And the building of temporary churches, a widespread activity that had been tolerated by the government, was halted by the police.

The effects of the pope's triumphal march through Poland remained long after he had returned to Rome. He bolstered the Polish church and strengthened the confidence of those who opposed the Communist regime.

There were reverberations throughout Eastern Europe. In Lithuania and the Ukraine, in Hungary and Czechoslovakia, anywhere the church was under seige, the pope's trip stirred new hope among the faithful.

In the months that followed his visit, more tangible results could be perceived. A new figure rose to challenge the

*Pope John Paul wipes away a tear following his farewell
speech in Cracow that ended his visit to Poland in 1979.
(United Press International)*

Communist regime. His name was Lech Walesa.

Walesa was the leader of the Solidarity movement, an organization of about fifty trade unions with almost ten million members. John Paul backed Walesa, occasionally telephoning him from the Vatican to offer his support.

In November 1980, when, after months of intense negotiation, the government recognized Solidarity, it marked the first time a Communist country had ever recognized a labor union independent of the country's own Communist Party. Lech Walesa headed the organization.

But Solidarity and the Communist Party were on a collision course. Late in the summer of 1981 a stern ultimatum was issued, not from Warsaw, but from Moscow. It demanded that the Polish government "immediately take determined and radical steps" against Solidarity. "The Soviet people . . . have the fundamental right to demand that an

Symbol of Poland's Solidarity movement became internationally known. (Polish Daily News)

end be put to the anti-Soviet impudence in Poland,'' the Kremlin stated. At the same time, Moscow scheduled military exercises involving thousands of troops along Poland's borders.

By his stirring visit to Poland and his support of Solidarity, the pope had shown he was a man of influence and power. His defiance was proving very troublesome to Communist authorities in Moscow. To more than a few of them he was a threat that would have to be dealt with.

CHAPTER

10

POPE JOHN PAUL'S VISIT TO THE UNITED STATES IN October 1979 was an enormous personal triumph. Millions of Americans endured hours of waiting and drenching rain to catch a glimpse of him. "Rarely before," said *Newsweek* magazine, "had anyone, visitor or native, commanded American crowds in such vast numbers, or moved them so visibly to exhilaration, solemnity, joy, and an outpouring of love."

The press and television were captivated by the pope. A cover story about John Paul in *Time* magazine called him a "superstar." *Newsweek* devoted two consecutive cover stories to the visit. *The New York Times,* one observer noted, "turned out feature stories by the pound." 'WE LOVED HIM' declared the *New York Daily News* on its front page.

Street vendors and hawkers sold pope buttons, pope mugs and key chains, pope posters, pope T-shirts ('I got a peek at the Pope'), and pope bumper stickers ('Come follow me—John Paul II'). There were souvenir books and booklets, John Paul II pennants, Vatican flags, and a record album of the pope singing a Polish folk song called "The Raftsman."

"There was something miraculous about the whole week," said Richard Threlkeld on CBS-TV. "There were times when we felt he was one of us and other times when we were simply in awe of him. You didn't have to be Catholic to admire him, to want to see him, be close to him. It was quite a week. Maybe America needed it. In the past twenty years our leaders have all either died on us or disappointed

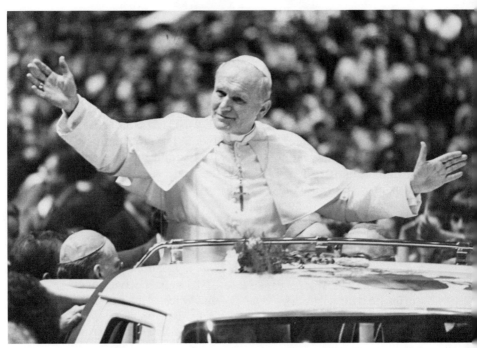

When John Paul visited the United States in 1979, Time *magazine called him a "Superstar."*
(Chris Sheridan)

us. One after another they have broken our hearts. This week we met somebody else.''

From the first day the trip was announced, it stirred hopes among American Catholics. Crisis and confusion had plagued the church for almost two decades. It was thought that perhaps the pope's visit would usher in a period of stability.

Many observers traced the turmoil within the church to the Second Vatican Council, which greatly affected the lives of American Catholics. The mass, which had always been said in Latin, was translated into English. Altars were turned around, and the priest now faced the congregation. Lay people could receive communion wafers in their own hands before consuming them. Women became lectors at mass and ministers of holy communion.

But the freedom granted Catholics by virtue of the Vatican Council triggered some enormous problems. One was dissent. In 1968 in his encyclical titled "Humanae Vitae"— "Human Life"—Pope Paul VI had restated the church's traditional teaching that the use of artificial birth control methods was "intrinsically evil." While some Catholics accepted the decision, many others ignored it, and "the pill" replaced rhythm as the typical Catholic method of family planning in the United States. And Catholic marriages were as likely to end in divorce as those of non-Catholics. Some surveys indicated that as many as four out of five churchgoing Catholics rejected the papal document.

Another problem facing the American Catholic Church was a serious shortage of priests. Since the Vatican Council, approximately 10,000 had left the priesthood. Church leaders hoped the visit of the pope would stimulate interest in the priestly life among young people.

The decrease in the number of priests led to a questioning of an all-male priesthood. If there was such a shortage, why not permit women to receive the Sacrament of Holy Orders and become priests?

Like priests, the number of American nuns had declined drastically. In 1966 there were 181,000 American nuns; by 1979 the figure had dropped to 131,000.

Whereas nuns had once confined their work to teaching or hospital duties, they now were involved in many fields of social service. They worked on behalf of the elderly and for prisoners' rights. They ran colleges and shelters for battered women. They campaigned against nuclear arms.

But many nuns still felt they lacked a voice in the affairs of the church. Being banned from the priesthood and other ministries was only a part of the problem. Their status—overall—was 'second class.'

Not long before the pope left Rome for the United States, it was announced from the Vatican that only priests would be allowed to distribute communion during the pope's masses here. Many women took the announcement as another slap at their hopes to gain equal recognition within the church.

The pope arrived in Boston, where he was met by Rosalynn Carter, wife of the President, and other dignitaries. The pope's motorcade traveled through the city, ending at Boston Common where he celebrated mass. He spent the night at the archbishop's residence, as he did in other cities he visited.

The next day in New York City, the pope spent most of his time at the United Nations, where he addressed the General Assembly. In the evening he celebrated mass at Yankee Stadium after first making calls at churches in Harlem and the South Bronx.

The following morning a remarkable scene unfolded at New York's Madison Square Garden, jammed to overflowing with 19,000 high school students. They greeted the pope with deafening cheers and applause; then, to welcome him, they sang "Follow Me," "I Am the Bread of Life," and the theme from "Star Wars." The pope was then presented with gifts—a guitar, a pair of jeans, handmade medallions, a photo of earth from outer space, and a T-shirt emblazoned

*The pope walks and chats with United Nations officials
before addressing UN General Assembly.
(Chris Sheridan)*

with the words "The Big Apple Welcomes Pope John Paul II."

The young people broke into nine minutes of spontaneous applause, whistles, and cheers before the pope could speak. Cardinal Cooke, seated beside the pope on the podium, tried to still the outburst but could not. As the clamor continued, the pope smiled and made a soft cooing sound—"Woooohh"—with which Polish parents often express ap-

Riding in his "popemobile," John Paul waves to crowd at New York's Yankee Stadium.
(Chris Sheridan)

proval of their children. *Newsweek* magazine called it a "boisterous love-in."

In Philadelphia, where he visited his good friend Cardinal Krol, the pope said mass before an enormous crowd at Logan Square. He stopped at the Ukrainian Cathedral of the Immaculate Conception the next morning and later offered a mass for priests at the Civic Center.

As the pope was speaking in Philadelphia, people of the Midwest were converging on Des Moines, Iowa, where he was to appear the next day. They came by foot and on bicycles, by car, camper, and bus.

The pope greets high school students at New York's Madison Square Garden. At right is Cardinal Terence Cooke of New York. (Chris Sheridan)

Although Des Moines is largely Protestant, the pope's visit there was supported by the community as a whole. Businesses lent secretaries to assist the diocese in preparing for the visit, and scores of individuals gave up their vacations to lend a hand. The diocese assumed the costs of the visit, except for those normally provided any visiting notable, such as security. Catholics were encouraged to make contributions toward the cost, estimated to be $1 million. When the call went out for funds, one of the first responses was from a local Methodist church with a contribution of $1,000.

After he arrived at the Des Moines airport, the pope was taken by helicopter to tiny Cumming, Iowa. Its 111 year-old whitewashed church, St. Patrick's, sits gracefully

Parochial-school students hail John Paul during his visit to New York City. (Chris Sheridan)

on an oak-shaded knoll overlooking rolling plains. The pope blessed the church and hailed the 200 or so parishioners for the closeness of their community and the simplicity of their life-styles. He said: "How privileged you are that, in such a setting, you can worship together."

Later, at an open-air mass, the pope told the congregation, "Conserve the land well, so that your children's children and generations after them will inherit an even richer land than was entrusted to you."

In Chicago the pope offered mass for the city's Polish community, then attended a special session of the United States Bishops' Conference. He celebrated mass at Grant Park and after dinner attended a concert by the Chicago Symphony Orchestra at Holy Name Cathedral.

Huge throngs greeted the pope everywhere. This is scene in Philadelphia's Logan Circle.
(Chris Sheridan)

John Paul's chartered airplane arrived from Chicago at
Andrews Air Force Base outside Washington in brilliant
sunshine. Vice President Walter Mondale greeted the pope,
praising him for having given Americans ''new hope and
new courage.''

A motorcade took the pope through the streets of
downtown Washington, and he then celebrated mass at St.
Matthews Cathedral. The throng that cheered loudly as he
entered the cathedral managed to overwhelm a cluster of

The pope celebrates mass in Philadelphia.
(Chris Sheridan)

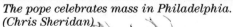

112

sign-bearing demonstrators who were protesting the pope's stand concerning the role of women in church affairs.

After lunch the pope was driven to a reception given by President Jimmy Carter. Some 5,000 guests, including members of Congress, assembled on the north and south lawns of the White House to be introduced to the pope. But first he had an hour-long private meeting with President Carter and then gave a brief address in which he called upon the United States to continue its efforts to halt the arms race, making specific reference to nuclear arms.

The fact that an American President, and a Southern Baptist, shook the hand of the pope in the White House and shared a speaker's platform with him marked a striking advance in the history of America's relationship with the Catholic Church, a relationship that had been riddled with conflict and bitterness. Between 1830 and 1860, when the United States was engulfed with great waves of immigrants from Europe, the Catholic population grew by leaps and bounds, increasing from 318,000 to 3,103,000. This sudden increase in the number of foreign-born Catholics gave rise to a form of prejudice known as nativism. Some native-born Americans mocked "Romish" beliefs and practices and questioned the loyalty and patriotism of Catholics through sensational newspapers, books, and lectures. Anti-Catholic resentment exploded in the burning of a convent in Charlestown, Massachusetts, in 1830, and in bloody riots in Philadelphia in 1844.

In politics nativism led to the formation of the Know-Nothing Party in the 1850s. When Pope Pius IX sent a block of Italian marble to be used in the construction of the Washington Monument, members of the Know-Nothing Party dumped it into the Potomac River.

Anti-Catholic bias began to diminish after the Civil War. But the America Protective Association in the 1890s and the Ku Klux Klan in the 1920s were other organizations that expressed anti-Catholic feeling.

In the presidential election of 1928, Herbert Hoover trounced Al Smith, a Catholic, in a landslide. Most observers said the election showed that a Catholic could never be elected President. Why, he might invite the pope to the White House!

Then came another Catholic presidential candidate, John Kennedy. In the campaign of 1960, Kennedy told an association of Houston ministers, "I believe in an America where the separation of Church and State is absolute, where no Catholic prelate would tell the President, should he be a Catholic, how to act, and no Protestant minister would tell his parishioners for whom to vote."

People believed what Kennedy said. When he defeated Richard Nixon and became President, he exploded the myth that no Catholic could ever claim this nation's highest office.

President Carter, in his welcome to the pope, noted that John Paul had come to the United States as a "poet, philosopher, and pastor." Pausing, he cocked his head and added, "But mostly, I think, as a pastor." Then grinning, he turned toward the pope and said, "Don't you agree?"

"You are right," the pope said.

After his meeting with President Carter, John Paul visited the headquarters of the Organization of American States, then met with diplomatic representatives of foreign nations who were stationed in Washington.

On the last day of the pope's visit, activist nuns planned a protest. The pope had refused to grand an audience during his visit to the Leadership Conference of Women Religious, the only organization of American sisters to be officially approved by the Vatican. Many nuns were also upset because the pope, in his speeches, rejected the idea of women as ordained priests. The nuns made pale blue armbands and handed them out before the pope's speech to 4,000 nuns at the National Shrine of the Immaculate Conception on the campus of the Catholic University of America in Washington. Some wanted to stage a walkout during the pope's speech as a way of showing how they felt about his stand on ordination. But this strategy was vetoed. Instead, about fifty nuns stood up when the pope began to speak and remained standing until he had finished.

Even stronger protest came from Sister Theresa Kane, a member of the Sisters of Mercy order and president of the Leadership Conference of Women Religious. Some observers gasped when Sister Theresa, wearing a neat brown suit with a lapel cross to symbolize her status as a nun, rose to challenge the pope, asking him to "be mindful of the intense suffering and pain which is part of the life of many women in the United States." Recalling the pope's own words concerning human dignity, she asked him to provide "the possibility of women as persons being included in all ministeries of our church."

The pope did not seem to know what to say or do at first. He raised his hands as if he wanted to interrupt her—but did not. Only about half of the nuns applauded Sister Theresa, and one, Mother Mary Sixtina from Alton, Illinois, paid for an advertisement in the *Washington Post* to apologize for Sister Theresa's "impertinent" remarks to the pope, noting that she has "also offended the millions of us who love him and gladly accept his teaching."

After his visit to Catholic University, the pope met with journalists and later celebrated mass on the Mall. A special altar was constructed in front of the headquarters of the Smithsonian Institution. That night the pope left for Rome.

While the pope had appeared warm and gentle to the millions who saw him, he issued a stern and unvarying message. He warned against materialism. He lectured against permissiveness. He spoke out against selfishness. These were among the most important of his statements:

The Priesthood
"Priesthood is forever . . . we do not return the gift once given. It can not be that God who gave the impulse to say 'yes' now wishes to hear 'no.' "

115

"The church's traditional decision to call men to the priesthood, and not to call women, is not a statement about human rights, nor an exclusion of women from holiness and mission in the church. Rather, this decision expresses the conviction of the church about this particular dimension of the gift of priesthood by which God has chosen to shepherd his flock."

Divorce

"With the candor of the Gospels, the compassion of pastors, and the charity of the Church, you [the bishops] faced the question of the indissolubility of marriage, rightly stating: 'The covenant between a man and a woman joined in Christian marriage is as indissoluble and irrevocable as God's love for his people and Christ's love for his church.' "

The pope and President Jimmy Carter share a laugh during John Paul's visit to Washington.
(Chris Sheridan)

Sexuality

"In today's society, we see so many disturbing tendencies and so much laxity regarding the Christian view on sexuality that all have one thing in common: recourse to the concept of freedom to justify any behavior. . . .

"Free indeed is the person who models his or her behavior in a responsible way according to . . . objective good."

Youth

"Dear Young People: do not be afraid of honest effort and honest work. With Christ's help, and through prayer, you can answer His call, resisting temptation and fads, and every form of mass manipulation."

Contraception and Abortion

"In exalting the beauty of marriage, you [the bishops] rightly spoke against both the ideology of contraception and contraceptive acts, as did the encyclical Humanae Vitae. And I myself today . . . ratify the teaching of this encyclical. . . .

"You also gave witness to the truth . . . serving all humanity, when . . . you reaffirmed the right to life and the inviolability of every human life, including the life of unborn children."

Wealth and Poverty

"Riches and freedom create a special obligation. The poor of the United States and the world are your brothers and sisters in Christ. You must never be content to leave them crumbs from the feast. You must take of your substance, and not just of your abundance, in order to help them. And you must treat them like guests at your family table."

In the weeks that followed his departure, many people sought to explain the great outpouring of love and enthusiasm for the pope. Some suggested that it was John Paul's

117

personality, that he possessed some special gift that enabled him to excite large numbers of people. Others suggested that his appeal was based on his skillful use of television and the press. Still others said that his popularity could be attributed to the traditional American desire to create and worship heroes.

Reverend Billy Graham, the noted Protestant minister and evangelist had another answer. "There is a spiritual hunger in this nation," he said, "a hunger which the visit of the pope clearly revealed."

Graham, writing in *The Saturday Evening Post,* explained how he had sensed the existence of this spiritual hunger for years. "I believe it is one of the most important realities of our time," he declared.

He described how people come up to him everywhere —in airplane terminals, hotel lobbies, restaurants, and television studios—and unburden their hearts. He said: "Their stories, of course, are different, and yet there is a common theme: 'I have a fine home, a good job, and economic security. But down deep inside I am empty. I need God. How can I find Him and fill the hunger in my heart?' "

Graham said that he was not surprised by the tumultuous welcome the pope received. "I believe a major reason for it is because the American people are yearning for answers to the deeper issues of life," he said, "answers which can only be found in God."

CHAPTER
11

IN HIS FIRST TWO-AND-ONE-HALF YEARS AS POPE, John Paul traveled the world. In addition to his visits to Mexico, Poland, and the United States, he went to Turkey and Brazil, to France and West Germany, and to six African nations. He charmed crowds everywhere with his open and warm-hearted style. He never shied away from physical contact with the throngs that pressed about him. He was beginning to be called the "people's pope."

Previous popes had limited themselves to receiving small groups of visitors in their Vatican quarters or to holding general audiences in a large auditorium within the Vatican complex. John Paul changed that. He moved the general audiences outdoors when weather permitted, holding them in St. Peter's Square. Many more people could thus attend.

Standing in his white, jeep-like vehicle, which the press had dubbed the *popemobile,* he would circle through the crowd dispensing blessings. Occasionally he would dismount and dive into the crowd to shake hands and kiss babies. Traffic along the Tiber River would become snarled as a result of the pope's appearance. Rome's mayor warned the Vatican of "inevitable sanctions" unless something was done to control the crowds.

One such audience was scheduled for late in the afternoon on May 13, 1981. The various wooden barricades that established the route of the popemobile through the crowded square were put in place. About 100,000 tourists and pilgrims were on hand.

A loud cheer went up from the crowd as the jeep entered the square, the pope standing, smiling, and waving. The vehicle circled slowly through the crowd. Shouts of *Viva il papa!* ("Long live the pope!") rang out.

The vehicle had completed one circuit through the crowd and was starting a second. The pope had finished hugging a baby and was reaching out to take the hand of a woman when four shots rang out. George and Virginia Beckam, tourists from California, were standing on chairs taking photographs of the pope. "One minute the pope was waving and smiling, and the next minute he wasn't there any more," Mr. Beckam was to say later. "It finally dawned on me that, my God, he had been shot."

Francesco Pasanisi, Inspector General of the Vatican police, was at the pope's side when the shots were fired. "I saw a mark, first small, like a scarlet rose on his white vestments," he would later tell the press. "When I jumped on the jeep and tried to hold him, he was going limp and sliding down." The pope had been wounded, as it turned out, in the lower abdomen, the right forearm, and the index finger of his left hand.

Pasanisi shouted "Go! Go!" to the pope's driver. "Meanwhile, the red stain was getting bigger," Pasanisi recalled. "My hands were wet with blood."

"And the pope said, 'thank you, thank you,' and 'courage, courage.' Imagine it—*he* was telling *me* to be calm and courageous."

An aide lifts the head of Pope John Paul following the assassination attempt in St. Peter's Square in May 1981. (United Press International)

In St. Peter's Square all was chaos. After the gunman had fired at the pope he had tried to run, tossing away his nine millimeter automatic pistol as he fled. But he got only a few yards before members of the crowd grabbed him and held him until the police arrived. They marched him off to police headquarters for questioning.

The stunned tourists and pilgrims milled about the square. Many of them wept. A voice eventually announced the news on the public address system. "The Holy Father has been wounded. Please pray for him."

Thousands of the faithful knelt, joining in the Lord's Prayer and Hail Mary. A group of Polish pilgrims sang hymns in the pope's native tongue.

An ambulance had been parked nearby, its engine running. The pope's vehicle lurched to a stop beside the ambulance. Its crew transferred the pope to a stretcher and lifted him into the ambulance. Its lights flashing, its siren wailing, the ambulance sped to Gemelli Hospital.

The wound in John Paul's abdomen continued to spurt blood. He remained barely conscious, mumbling in Polish.

The ambulance pulled up to the emergency entrance of Gemelli Hospital. The trip had taken about twenty minutes. "It's the pope! It's the pope," the driver cried out to a nurse. The pope was wheeled into the hospital.

Doctors in the emergency room quickly discovered that three bullets had struck the pope, one in the left hand and a second in the right arm. The third penetrated John Paul's stomach, producing multiple wounds to the large and small intestine and the lower part of the colon.

The pope was on the operating table for five-and-one-half hours. He received six pints of blood, about three-fifths of the body's normal volume. He was given massive doses of antibiotics. By midnight the pope was in the recovery room and fully conscious.

The pope's recovery was slowed by the development of a serious viral infection. But after a second major operation, he began to show steady improvement. He convalesced at Castel Gondolfo during the late summer and autumn of 1981.

People were not only shocked by the assassination attempt, they were dismayed by it. Why would anyone want to shoot a man who had traveled the world searching for peace and human rights? In the years since the shooting, that question has been answered, at least in part.

At the very time the pope was beginning to undergo the surgery needed to repair the serious abdominal wounds he had suffered, the police were already interrogating the gunman, a tall and gaunt twenty-three-year-old Turk named Mehmet Ali Agca. The oldest of three children, Agca was born in 1958 near Malatya. His father died when he was very young. Agca was a bright student, but he dropped out of school at fifteen. He joined a street gang and began running errands for local crime bosses. He was later used as a truck driver by individuals smuggling heroin out of Turkey.

In 1977, at the urging of a former schoolmate from Malatya, Agca went to the Middle East—to Syria, Israel, and Lebanon. In Beirut, Lebanon, he received instruction at a secret Palestinian guerilla training camp.

Agca's trial in Rome in July that year lasted only seventy-two hours. His lawyer made no effort to establish his client's innocence. Instead, he tried to get Agca a light sentence by arguing that he was a religious fanatic. The court deliberated seven hours, then gave Agca a lifetime sentence, the maximum permitted under Italian law.

The trial shed little light on Agca's motives. He described himself as an international terrorist dedicated to terrorism of any kind. He said that "the decision to shoot the pope was mine, and no one asked me to do it."

But Agca did not act alone. Evidence now exists that links Agca with the Bulgarian secret police in a plot that possibly involves the Soviet Union's top leadership.

The conspiracy first came to light through an article that appeared in the September 1982 edition of the *Reader's Digest*. Titled "The Plot to Murder the Pope," the article was written by Claire Sterling, an authority on international terrorism and the author of a highly regarded book, *The Terror Network*. Not long after, NBC Television, in an hour-long documentary, also pointed out Agca's connection with the Bulgarian secret police and the likelihood that the plot was directed by the Soviets. Said NBC-TV's Marvin Kalb: "The pope is described by those in the Vatican who know him best as believing that the Russians were behind Agca's attempt to kill him, and they may try again."

Italian investigators have gathered enough evidence to indicate that Agca was part of a conspiracy. At the scene of the crime, St. Peter's Square, Agca had at least two accomplices. One was photographed from behind by a television cameraman as he fled with a gun in his hand. A second was seen racing for a bus after the shots had been fired. Italian authorities were able to establish that this second man was Omar Ay, who, like Agca himself, was a terrorist fugitive.

They were further able to establish that Ay had been provided with a counterfeit Turkish passport on the same day Agca had received one. Indeed, their passports bore consecutive numbers, 136635 and 136636.

Additional evidence that points to the existence of a plot came from notes found in Agca's pockets at the time of his arrest. The notes were instructions from someone who played a leadership role in Agca's activities in the days just before the shooting. "Choose a bag carefully," ordered one of the notes. Authorities believed that this referred to the bag in which Agca carried the bulky revolver into St. Peter's Square. "Hair dye is essential," said another note. Hair dye was found in Agca's hotel room.

Investigators also obtained evidence from Agca himself during his questioning. They gradually pieced together a scenario of events leading to the assassination attempt.

The story had its beginning on February 1, 1979, with the killing of Abdi Ipekci, an outspoken Turkish newspaper editor who supported liberal causes. Several months later, Agca was arrested for the murder. "I did it; I killed Ipekci," Agca freely admitted. He said that he had gotten the murder weapon from the notorious Gray Wolf organization, a German youth group with Nazi connections. Agca, it is said, was thus seeking to associate himself with the far right, with fascism.

Agca was sent to prison for murder. One day late in November 1979, Agca escaped by simply walking out of the prison. He had to pass through no less than eight doors, which ordinarily would have been locked. He obviously had to have been helped by prison authorities, which meant that large bribes were undoubtedly paid.

After his escape Agca was provided with a fake passport and entered Bulgaria, Turkey's neighbor to the north. Many of the countries of Eastern Europe, including Hungary, Yugoslavia, Romania, and Albania, are satellite nations of the Soviet Union. But Bulgaria is more closely allied to the Soviets than any of the others. Violent operations

Mehmet Ali Agca of Turkey, the man who shot and wounded Pope John Paul II. (United Press International)

planned in Moscow are often carried out by Bulgarian terrorist bands. The K.G.B., the Soviet intelligence agency, is known to be in direct control of the Bulgarian security police.

Agca stayed in Bulgaria for almost two months. He took up residence in a first-class hotel in Sofia, Bulgaria's capital. He entered the country penniless. He departed with $50,000 in cash.

After leaving Bulgaria Agca traveled through much of Europe, never staying long in any one country. He eventually registered as a student in Perugia, in central Italy. He later took up residence in Rome, using the guesthouse in which he lived as the base of operations for his attack upon the pope.

The link between Agca and Moscow was confirmed in 1981. Iordan Mantarov, a Bulgarian official who had abandoned his country that year, told French intelligence officials that the plot to kill the pope was devised by the K.G.B. and the Bulgarian secret service.

Why? Why would the Soviet leadership plot the murder of the pope?

Because, according to Mantarov, the K.G.B. believed that the pope was essential to a plot being formed by the United States to overthrow the Communist government of Poland. Mantarov said he had been told by a high-ranking Bulgarian official that the K.G.B. believed that the election of Karol Wojtyla had been engineered by Zbigniew Brzezinski, who, at the time, was serving as national security advisor to President Jimmy Carter. Once Cardinal Wojtyla had been established as pope, Brzezinski would be better able to take advantage of the unrest in Poland and lure the country out of the Communist orbit—at least that is what the K.G.B. is thought to have theorized.

Interestingly, Brzezinski is one of the few American officials who have stated that the Soviet Union was involved in the shooting of Pope John Paul. "I'm reasonably satisfied that there was some sort of Turkish-Bulgarian connection," Brzezinski said in an interview with *The New York Times* early in 1983. "In turn," he added, "anything of that historic magnitude couldn't have been undertaken by Bulgaria without the knowledge of the Soviet Union."

The theory becomes more believable when one looks at the events that were taking place in Poland in the summer of 1980. The shipyard workers of Gdansk were demonstrating to protest the fact that the Communist unions did not truly represent them. Poland's puppet government was seeking the assistance of armed forces from other Eastern bloc countries and even from the Soviet Union itself in order to put an end to the strikes. There were fears that the unrest might spread to the Ukraine, a republic of the Soviet Union's in southern Europe, just east of Poland.

The strikes and unrest eventually led to the birth of Solidarity, the first independent union ever to come to power in a Soviet-controlled nation. Lech Walesa, the leader of the union, was raised to national prominence. The torch of freedom was beginning to burn.

To the Soviets John Paul was looked upon as the spiritual father of Solidarity. Certainly the trade union could never have been born without his blessing. For this reason, it has been theorized, someone holding a high official position in the Soviet Union decided that the pope would have to be killed.

Agca himself declared in July 1983 that the Soviet secret police and the Bulgarian secret service took part in the plot to kill the pope. It was the first time that he had made such a statement.

"I have been in Bulgaria; I stayed several times," he said in an exchange with reporters.

"I have been trained—by K.G.B. I have been trained by special experts in international terrorism."

If Agca and Mantarov are to be believed, then the decision to assassinate the pope had to involve Yuri Andropov, the man who headed the K.G.B. at the time. In November 1982, when Leonid Breshnev died, Andropov succeeded him as the ruler of the Soviet Union.

Soviet officials have of course denied any direct involvement in the assassination attempt. They have branded such accusations as "a campaign totally steeped in lies."

Late in May 1982, the pope visited Portugal. He rode in an open limousine through the streets of Lisbon as throngs cheered. By the time he had reached his destination, the Lisbon cathedral, the car was inches deep in confetti and flower petals the crowd had showered on him. The same day, the pope met with the president of Portugal, Antonio Ramalho Eanes.

The highlight of the pope's visit to Portugal was to be a mass at the shrine of Our Lady of Fatima. Fatima itself is a hamlet in western Portugal. It was at Fatima in 1917 that three shepherd children are said to have seen six apparitions of the Virgin Mary.

The pope was going to Fatima to fulfill a vow of gratitude he had made to the Virgin Mary for having saved his life a year earlier when he was shot in St. Peter's Square. The assassination attempt occurred on the same day, May 13, and almost at the same time that the shepherd children claimed to have seen the first of the apparitions of the Virgin Mary.

To John Paul, his escape from death and his eventual recovery were the result of the Blessed Virgin's intervention. "It all happened to me that day," he told a group of visitors to the Vatican several months after the shooting. "I have seen the extraordinary maternal protection that showed itself to be more powerful than homicidal bullets."

Pope John Paul's mass was to mark the anniversary of the apparitions. More than half a million pilgrims were expected to be in attendance.

On the evening before the mass, the pope visited the shrine. Carrying a candle, he was mounting the altar steps when suddenly a man wielding a sixteen-inch bayonet charged him. A security guard wrestled the man to the ground, but not before he came within an arm's length of the pope. The pope was jostled in the skirmish, but continued moving up the stairs to the altar.

The next morning at the anniversary mass the pope seemed to be making a reference to the second assassination attempt when he referred to the "menace of evil" that he saw spreading through the world. He called upon the Madonna for deliverance "from famine and war . . . from sin against the life of man . . . from hatred . . . from every kind of injustice in life and of society."

The man who had brandished the bayonet was later identified as Fernandez y Krohn, a thirty-two-year-old Spanish priest, a fanatical opponent of the reforms established by the Second Vatican Council. Tried for the crime, he was given a prison term of seven years and one month.

Not long after the attack, Pope John Paul remarked to an old friend, "This is not the first attempt on the life of the pope." Then he added, "Nor will it be the last."

CHAPTER
12

POPE JOHN PAUL'S DOCTORS ADVISED HIM NOT TO travel for a year. But just nine months after the bullets from Mehmet Ali Agca's pistol struck him down in St. Peter's Square, John Paul was off on a grueling eight-day visit to West Africa.

The Catholic Church in the West African countries he visited—Nigeria, Benin, Gabon, and Equatorial Guinea—was growing by leaps and bounds. John Paul's aim in making the pilgrimage was to bolster the spirit and resolve of the faithful and at the same time strengthen ties with Christianity's chief rival in West Africa—Islam, the religious faith of the Muslims.

Later in 1982, when Argentina went to war with Great Britain over the Falkland Islands, the pope sought to act as a peacemaker. He visited both warring nations and met with three heads of state—Queen Elizabeth II in London, President Ronald Reagan at the Vatican, and Argentine President Leopoldo Galtieri in Buenos Aires—in his role as a troubleshooting diplomat.

John Paul also visited Switzerland, Spain, and San Marino, a tiny republic in eastern Italy.

He began the next year, 1983, with a journey to Central America. Almost all of the nations he visited there—Costa Rica, Guatemala, Panama, Honduras, Belize, El Salvador, Nicaragua, and Haiti—were beset by poverty and violence. There were fears for the pope's physical safety.

It is not likely that John Paul hoped to solve the grave economic and social problems of these nations. His goal may have been set forth in a speech he delivered to a rally of young people at Costa Rica's national stadium. He told them: "You, my beloved children, have the grave responsibility to break the chain of hate . . . You must create a better world than that of your ancestors. If you don't, blood will continue to run, and tomorrow the tears will give witness to the sorrows of your children." John Paul's hope was to plant the seeds of change.

The pope makes his way through a crowd attending mass in Ibaden, Nigeria, during his 8-day visit to Africa in 1980. (United Press International)

The pope has traveled many thousands of miles in the first four-and-one-half years of his papacy, far more than any of his predecessors. He has been called the most popular pope in history. But John Paul is more than just popular. He has aroused an outpouring of affection and trust that no political leader in the world can hope to inspire.

In April 1983, ABC Television News presented a one-hour special titled, "The Pope and His Vatican." In producing the program, ABC interviewers and cameramen were granted access to John Paul and to many of the people who work for him. During the telecast, Bill Blakemore, the narrator of the production, asked the pope, "Holy Father, some people say you are traveling too much."

"Yes. I am convinced," the pope answered.

"You are?" said Blakemore, somewhat surprised.

"I am convinced I am traveling too much," the pope said again. "But sometimes it's necessary to do something of what is too much."

It was inevitable that John Paul's travels would take him back to Poland. The trip took place in mid-1983.

The situation in Poland in 1983 was much different from what it had been when he had visited the country in 1979. That trip had helped to bring Solidarity into existence. But the government had felt threatened by Solidarity, by the anti-government strikes and demonstrations it had fostered and by its call for nationwide balloting to test the popularity of the Communist Party.

When the government decided to crack down, it did so quickly and efficiently. General Wojciech Jaruzelski imposed martial law on Poland twelve days before Christmas in 1981. Troops were sent into the streets. Thousands were arrested, and hundreds were killed as militiamen broke up strikes or sit-ins at factories and mines. Telephone lines were cut. Travel was restricted. Solidarity was officially outlawed.

Martial law was still in effect when the pope returned to Poland in June 1983. Hundreds of political prisoners remained in government custody.

John Paul called his journey a "pilgrimage of hope." Its ambition was to boost the morale of the dispirited Poles and to keep alive the ideals of personal freedom that martial law had all but extinguished.

The chief religious reason for the pope's trip was to celebrate the 600th anniversary of the Black Madonna, Poland's holiest icon.

In the days before the pope's arrival at Czestochowa, people streamed into the city. About one million attended the outdoor mass the pope celebrated at the shrine. He expressed his gratitude "for all the evidence of solidarity that my countrymen . . . have shown me in the difficult period of the last months." At the mention of the word "solidarity," the throng applauded and banners shot up emblazoned with the name of the outlawed trade union. "SOLIDARITY LIVES" said one.

The pope's visit took him to Warsaw, where he celebrated a mass in memory of Cardinal Stefan Wyszynski, who had died in 1981. He also traveled to Nowa Huta, where, as Archbishop of Cracow, he had led much of the battle to build the steel-mill town's first church. He dedicated yet another church at Nowa Huta, the town's sixth. Three more churches were under construction.

Earlier, at an open-air mass in Cracow, the pope attracted an estimated two million people, the largest crowd of the tour. He visited Wroclaw in western Poland, where he said mass at the mountain shrine of St. Anne. He also celebrated an open-air mass at Poznan and met with the local clergy.

While the pope's visit was intended to provide the Polish people with a spiritual lift, it was also intended to have a political effect. John Paul called for "social reform" in Poland and an end to the "severe rigors" of martial law. He met twice with General Jaruzelski, the Polish ruler, and once with Lech Walesa, head of the outlawed Solidarity union.

In the weeks that followed the pope's visit, the press

132

speculated on what the trip had accomplished. Perhaps the results were best summed up by Cardinal John Krol of Philadelphia, who accompanied the pope on the eight-day journey. Meeting with reporters on his return to the United States, the cardinal said: "I have a personal impression that there is, on the part of the regime, a desire to get back to normalcy, to get back to reform and a renewal, to get back to the business of working for the common good of all the people."

But real change, if it does occur, is not going to happen overnight. "The situation in Poland," as one Polish priest has noted, "can be resolved only through long, hard work, through patience, peace, and reason."

Changes that the pope may have hoped to have seen in the United States, and that he called for on his journey here, have not occurred either. Most Catholics continue to reject "natural" birth control in favor of contraceptives. Catholic marriages end in divorce about as often as those of non-Catholics. Women within the Catholic Church continue to seek permission to become ordained priests, while the shortage of priests grows more serious.

The pope, however, has no thought of changing his stand on these or any other moral or ethical issues. He held fast in the face of Nazi oppression. He boldly confronted Communism for thirty years. Indeed, as pope, he caused so much anxiety among Communist leaders that it may almost have cost him his life. Yet he has no intention of softening his stand on Communism, as his visit to Poland in 1983 confirms.

The pope sees the United States as threatened by a philosophy that he believes is every bit as evil as Communism. He refers to it as "consumerism." Consumerism places too great an emphasis on "things," on material objects and needs, on getting and spending.

The pope is just as much a foe of consumerism as he is of Communism. He will not make the slightest change to accommodate either in his basic philosophy.

The pope chats with Polish leader General Wojciech Jaruzelski during visit to Poland in 1983. (United Press International)

Pope John Paul's portrait is part of the scene during the
Pulaski Day Parade in New York City. (George Sullivan)

Because of consumerism, he fears that the people of the United States may be losing sight of their moral and spiritual values. Social chaos could be the result. As he told an audience in Dublin, Ireland, in 1979, "When the moral fiber of a nation is weakened, when the sense of personal responsibility is diminished, then the door is open for the manipulation of the many by the few. The challenge that is already with us is the temptation to accept as true freedom what in reality is only a new form of slavery."

To the young people of the world, to the young people of the United States, in particular, the pope has issued a special call. " 'Follow me!' " he has said, quoting from the Gospel of St. Mark. "Walk in my path! Stand by my side! Remain in my love!"

The pope has noted that many people "try to escape from their responsibility . . . in selfishness . . . in sexual pleasure . . . in drugs . . . in violence . . . in indifference . . . and in cynical attitudes."

Young student from New Jersey, dressed in native Polish costume, hails Solidarity during New York's Pulaski Day Parade in 1983. (George Sullivan)

"I propose to you the option of love, which is the opposite of escape," he says. "If you really accept that love from Christ, it will lead you to God—perhaps in the priesthood or religious life, perhaps in some special service to your brothers or sisters, especially to the needy, the poor, the lonely, the abandoned, those whose rights have been trampled upon, or those whose basic needs have not been provided for.

"Whatever you make of your life, let it be something that reflects the love of Christ."

The pope will continue to travel and speak in this vein. His voice will keep reminding the people of the world of their responsibilities to themselves, to one another, and to a higher spiritual power—to God.